How to be Human

How to be Human

By K. A. Leeman

For enquiries contact the publisher's website: www.kaleeka.com

ISBN 978-1-897573-11-2

First printing, 2010

Kaleeka Press

About the author...

K.A. Leeman was born in Montreal, Canada, the youngest in a Swiss immigrant family. After completing a degree in English and Education at Queen's University, K.A. Leeman worked and lived in Europe for several years, rediscovering her roots. She started Kaleeka Press in 2001; writing and publishing language Educational programs primarily in French and Spanish. She has also become a certified hypnotherapist and NLP practitioner and offers personal growth seminars and consulting in Toronto, Ontario.

Your spirit was alive before it came to LIFE

Free of all weight,

Both physical and emotional.

It danced and flowed in perfect elegance

With all the brightest of lights.

There was no darkness and no pain.

Suffering was inconceivable in the heavens

And even those who had heard of it

Could have no comprehension of it.

This is the story of one spirit,

On the journey of LIFE.

Contents

1

Book of Pearls

The heavens danced with the most beautiful lights – spirits who were vibrant and alive. There were no mornings for there were no nights. All was bright and darkness was unknown among them. They'd heard stories about the darkness, but as quickly as the stories were told, the residue of darkness in them would vanish into light. No heaviness could settle where only light and laughter lived. No darkness could penetrate when all was bright. No pain could be understood by those who felt none. Death was a word without meaning in the heavens. Its sadness could not take hold because it did not exist. And so the stories of darkness that were told were just as quickly forgotten. For no spirit living in bliss could even look upon grief with any understanding.

Ai, the Great Creator, would simply speak and things formed in front of him. He loved the bright lights of heaven and the dancing music they created for everyone. For Ai was so brilliant that his light touched even the remotest parts of heaven. But Ai saw something the spirits could not see. He saw their lights fading. He alone knew why their lights faded and he knew of a way to revitalize them. Of course light could be sustained for all eternity, but without wisdom its clarity and brilliance would begin to fade.

In reality the lights had not faded, but Ai could see all things before their time and he knew all things before they were created. So Ai created a sanctuary far away from the heavens. It was called LIFE. Each of the spirits would have to make a journey through LIFE to gain wisdom. And through LIFE, wisdom would be able to create a deep hole in the spirits. At first they could not understand how this hole could be a good thing but the Great Creator knew that the deeper the hole, the more light could be absorbed by it. And the heavens were filled with light. Spirits with the deepest holes, could truly offer the brightest light.

Ai knew what must be done, but he would not send the spirits away to experience LIFE without their agreement. In order for the journey to take root in their inner core, they would need to accept it fully. So as they accepted the journey of LIFE, they were each given the freedom to choose the experiences that would forge a deep hole in their spirits.

Initially the spirits were not sure about taking the journey, and Ai knew they would be reluctant. For who among them would choose to leave the wonders of heaven for darkness and pain, even for a fleeting moment, which was, in fact, LIFE? So Ai gathered them together and presented the greatest story they had ever heard – the story of Ai. None had ever heard his story, and as they pressed in to hear him speak, they radiated with his everlasting light. When he spoke, the fire within him became more radiant and warmed the entire celestial expanse. Light enveloped them and the great expanse became more brilliant.

After Ai finished telling his story, he showed them something that changed their minds – his own massive hole. Yes, Ai had forged a hole in his spirit. They realized that the brilliance of his light was due to the hole that had been created by his journey. When the spirits saw his hole they became eager to go themselves. They knew that having their own hole would increase their light too. Not only would they be able to shine more brightly, but also their understanding would be complete and their joy pure. And the object of pure joy was to shine so brightly as to have the feeling of exploding but without destruction.

Ai knew a greater mystery about the journey that he did not share with them. It was a mystery to be revealed by the journey itself. There were no words to describe it. It would be unraveled, however, in the course of the LIFE, but not for everyone. So the truth of the great mystery remained unspoken, even by those to whom it was revealed. Indeed the greatest mystery cannot be told. It can only be revealed through LIFE.

Terran was an eager spirit with the zest of many energies. He was the first to request entry into the sanctuary of LIFE. Ai was pleased with Terran's eagerness. He took Terran with him up to the heights – a loftier place where the quiet spirits liked to roam. Other spirits didn't know much about the quiet spirits except that they were warm and abounded in love. But because they roamed in the lofty heights of heaven they were rarely seen about the great expanse. Whenever Ai was about to do a new thing in the heavens he would often spend time in the lofty heights, formulating his thoughts. But most of the time Ai hovered freely in the heavens among all the spirits who made him laugh with their brilliant ideas.

So Ai took Terran up to the lofty heights and there, on a crest of vapors, appeared a book. It wasn't bound the way an ordinary book is bound. In fact it didn't look like a book at all. It was an assortment of countless images piled upon each other. Terran scanned over the floating images at light speed. There were so many he wanted to choose, but he realized while standing there that he could not choose with his thoughts. He had to choose with his heart. He had to let his heart guide him. Ai stepped back and allowed Terran the time and space to make his choices. One by one, the images were chosen. Whenever he saw one that felt right, Terran would reach out and the image would transform into a beautiful pearl and fall into his hand.

After his choices had been made, Terran stepped back and showed Ai the great quantity of pearls he'd been given. Ai smiled at him and blew over the pearls. Then, as if they had a mind of their own, the pearls joined together to form a beautiful circular pattern, each connecting to the next. Ai took the chain of pearls and placed it on Terran's head.

"These are the pearls you will take with you on your journey into LIFE. They will teach you what you need to learn while you are there. Do not despise them for they are precious. Each one will help dig out a hole in your spirit. Remember that you asked for each of these pearls. This is your chosen crown."

Terran listened soberly and made an agreement to care for the pearls and carry each one throughout his journey of LIFE. And so, each spirit had a chance to go up to the lofty heights and look into the book that sat upon the crest of vapors.

The book became known as the BOOK OF LIFE but some spirits liked to call it the BOOK OF PEARLS. The crest of vapors, which held up the BOOK OF LIFE, became known as the LOFTY SEAT, or the THRONE. Each spirit became increasingly excited in anticipation of his approach to the THRONE. The excitement of entering into an adventure that would lead to possessing more light was something almost too wonderful to comprehend. The spirits were excited about the images or pearls they chose and could hardly wait to have their turn. Ai was pleased to see the spirits revel in the adventure they would find in the sanctuary and he was even more pleased knowing they would learn about the mystery. The excitement roused the heavens as each spirit descended into the sanctuary to begin his journey.

At one point while Ai was assisting a spirit with his turn at the crest of vapors, he spied Oron hovering by the fountains of light. The fountains were glorious, pulsing with the most pleasing vibrations of sound as they shot upward and then descended in an intricate dance, dropping and swirling into a golden pool. All the while, rays of light fell upon each other in a magical sequence of glittering shimmers. The fountains were truly amazing to listen to and watch.

Spirits created them in an attempt to harness light into particular patterns. The heavens were filled with many such wonderful creations made by the spirits. Each inspired creation was made of light that could be harnessed in an infinite array of colors and vibrations, giving motion to the fountains. Vibrations of sound were everywhere in heaven. They were natural rhythms and melodies woven into everything that was alive with light and energy. Whenever the spirits created a new fountain or work, vibrations would dance their way in and through the creation. It was a wonderful byproduct of working with light.

Ai approached the hovering spirit as he meditated upon the fountain. Ai felt a hesitation around Oron's light.

"Are you contemplating your journey?" Ai already knew the answers to every question. His purpose in asking was only to ignite thought. For thought brought clarity and created a pathway that inevitably led to the answers. Ai knew he was evaluating the relevance of a LIFE journey. He was, in fact, wondering whether it was necessary to even take the journey at all. Ai could feel Oron's hesitation.

"What is the first experience of LIFE?" Oron asked his question without taking his focus away from the fountain.

"Darkness."

Ai spoke with a gentle voice, but the word itself gave Oron a strange feeling. He did not understand what darkness was exactly, but the absence of light was the absence of everything he knew.

"How can I exist in this "LIFE" sanctuary without light?"

"The sanctuary has no light of its own, so it cannot give you any. It's cold there, but you will enter into a warm dark shell. And the shell you'll be cast into must learn how to live. It will know nothing. As you enter and give it breath, your light will offer to be its guide."

Oron thought how strange it seemed to be trapped inside a shell, unable to move as freely as he did now.

"What is darkness like?"

"It will make you feel invisible – like you don't even exist."

Suddenly Oron burst into laughter. He couldn't imagine feeling or even thinking that.

"That's impossible! We are constantly bursting with our own essence and our joy is passed to one another without thought. I can't believe for a moment that anyone would think they were invisible."

"You speak this way because you live in the truth. Here there is only truth. But in LIFE there is darkness and in darkness, truth must hide for its light is not welcome there. Oron, because you are light, you cannot understand darkness. But you will." Ai turned away slowly. He waited momentarily for Oron to follow.

"Are you ready?" asked Ai. He knew the answer. He knew Oron was ready, but he needed to hear himself say it.

The source of all creation was conceived in thought and then birthed into words. Ai knew the power of words. Ai knew that to speak was to create and so the spoken word was a more powerful weapon than any. And the most powerful words were those that struck the heart. There within the heart the sanctuary was where the spirit would dwell. And the human heart was indeed the source from which all creation and destruction would certainly be conceived.

"Yes," he answered, "Let me choose my pearls and overcome this darkness you speak of." They ascended to the lofty heights and stood before the BOOK OF PEARLS. Standing in front of the BOOK, Oron watched the images appear and disappear quickly one after the other. He waited until he saw one that struck his heart. Then he saw it. It was the image of a woman sitting in a dimly lit room. She was wearing an apron, and wringing her hands in a dishtowel. She was looking into space not aware of her surroundings, but lost in a memory. Her cheeks were stained with clear lines from water that had fallen from her eyes. Oron was mesmerized by her expression. It was sad and weary. The water stains on her cheeks – something he'd never seen before, intrigued him. What did it mean? As he watched the woman, he felt something deep within begin to expand. Without hesitation, he reached out to touch the water on the woman's face and instantly the entire image shrank to the size of a small pearl and dropped into his hand. The image was so real and powerful that Oron could think of nothing else. It moved him in a way nothing had before. And he froze, unable to move forward in his thoughts. Ai touched his brow and instantly Oron felt warmth envelop him. He glanced up at Ai and relaxed again.

Oron knew this journey would certainly be a fascinating one and he became eager to engage more images from the BOOK OF LIFE. He passed over many images and so collected his pearls as the other spirits had done before him.

The visit to the crest of vapors was an experience Ai shared with every spirit. He knew the trials of the journey would be completely foreign to their understanding. He also knew it was important to assure them he would always be there with them, from the first pearl that dropped into their hand until the very last breath they would draw in LIFE.

2

The Journey into Life

Breezes, in the great expanse, were warm and carried with them an infinite variety of colors and fragrances. It was not unusual to see rainbows of color shimmering on currents of air, bending and swirling here and there. Spirits enjoyed floating along beside them breathing in their wonderful aromas. The exhilarating blend of fragrances was indescribably exquisite and the variations endless.

Now that Oron had his pearls, he was anticipating his turn to descend into LIFE. He couldn't imagine LIFE being so much different from here. The spirits who returned were clearly different than they were before they left. They seemed stronger and definitely brighter, and their eyes were different. He thought it must have been the knowledge of the mystery that changed them. LIFE must have been amazing to affect them so visibly. But Oron couldn't even imagine what it was going to be like. He noticed some spirits returned with markings. Oron wasn't sure what they were, but Ai had some markings too and he wore them with great fondness. Spirits who hadn't taken the journey were noticeably less bright and certainly lacked in other ways that were difficult to define. Oron noticed in the eyes of those who had returned, that they had a quiet serenity that was both beautiful and mysterious. Looking directly at them, he could sense their warmth even from a distance, the same way he could with Ai, and he loved being around them because of that feeling.

The mystery of the sanctuary experience was truly evident in the spirits touched by LIFE, but oddly none spoke of it. The more time Oron spent with the LIFE spirits, as they became known, the more excited he was about his own journey. With each passing breeze, Oron grew more focused on his imminent journey. He wanted to be like the LIFE spirits who seemed more complete, even though they all returned with holes and some of them with marks. But it was not yet his time.

After drifting on an exhilarating breeze, he could wait no longer and went to talk to Ai. Oron found him at the crest of vapors, reviewing a sequence of images. Ai sensed his approach and asked him a question before Oron even had a chance to say a word,

"Is there anything else you would like to know about LIFE before you descend?"

Indeed Oron had questions, but he was so eager to go that he'd put his questions aside knowing they would be answered soon enough. Now he stopped to search his heart again and found them.

"Why did you create the sanctuary of LIFE when everything here is perfect?"

Ai took great care in preparing and altering the sequence for each spirit's selection. It was important to plant the right seeds into the BOOK so that the images could truly grow into pearls when chosen by heart. And Ai was a master image-maker.

As he did with everything that came from nothing, Ai created with words. He needed only to speak, and it was. His hands didn't form anything. They were for holding and embracing. For Ai was the ultimate being. His energy was, in fact, pure love. And the hands of pure love were for reaching out. Words were the tools he used for creation and power and so speaking was always done with great premeditation.

"Because LIFE offers something more than perfection." He answered.

Oron was confused. How could anything offer more than perfection? Perfection was the completeness of everything. There was no state of existence that could be better. Everyone knew that. And everyone loved perfection.

"How?" he asked.

With a smile, Ai touched Oron's cheek. One touch from Ai sent a surge of warmth through Oron's being, filling him with exhilaration. Oron laughed, not sure why, but likely because it was a natural response to being touched by the hand of pure love.

"That's something you will learn in LIFE. It's a lesson that can never be taught in words, even my words. It must be learned in the journey. And the lesson will be yours alone to learn. Something you will share with no other spirit. But every spirit will share in. Although I am the Great Creator, I take pleasure in seeing the mystery create itself in you. Because then it will truly be yours. As much as you will create it, the mystery will also create you – it will inspire a transformation in you. In time you'll understand."

So often Ai spoke in riddles. But it wasn't intentional. It was just that usually the nature of what he tried to explain was so all encompassing, it was difficult to describe simply. And yet once understood, so many deep things were entirely simple. And that was always true with Ai. A low threshold of understanding obscured the simplest truths.

Oron wasn't overly concerned with the deeper truths, nor was he all that anxious to learn about the mystery. He trusted Ai's assurance that the mystery would be revealed soon enough. Right now he was more concerned about the darkness. Oron loved the light of heaven as much or more than other spirits did, so how could he live apart from that?

"How can I avoid the darkness of LIFE?"

Ai was not surprised by the question, but actually pleased. He knew this would be something particularly difficult for Oron given his nature.

"You can't. It will consume you."

"Then what is the purpose of LIFE?"

"To be consumed."

"I don't understand."

"Right now you're flooded with light. There is no distant place you can go where the light of heaven cannot touch you. But in the LIFE sanctuary, darkness is everywhere and it gives birth to a dark thing – a thing called fear. This fear can easily take root and permeate every place, just as the light does here. It will want to rule over your journey through LIFE."

"So what am I to learn?"

"You will learn what it is to experience darkness."

"And how can I overcome it?" asked Oron, now a bit disappointed.

"You may not. But if you choose to, you can find a path of light even in the darkness." Something then occurred to Oron that he hadn't considered before. The realization of it made him feel cold. It was a feeling he hadn't experienced before.

"Will you be there?"

"No."

Ai saw the expression on Oron's face. This realization made him very uncomfortable. Ai wanted to tell him more, but chose his words carefully.

"I will still talk to you just like I am now. The problem is you won't be able to hear me clearly. The darkness of LIFE is very effective and it will be difficult for you to hear or even find me. But if you first explore the sanctuary closely, you'll recognize my fingerprint in everything," he smiled. "And that will lead you to find yourself, because you will forget who you are. But when you find yourself, you'll find me. It won't be easy to do because the darkness will blind and confuse you. You'll find the sanctuary to be a turbulent place. And you'll feel the distinct coldness of my absence. And that part will be difficult for you."

There was so much about LIFE that was intriguing to Oron and at the same time overwhelming. He had no idea what it would be like not to be able to see and feel Ai's presence all the time. What a strange thought – strange but not impossible.

"So LIFE is like wearing a blindfold. I'll just have to rely on what I know to be true without seeing or feeling it."

"You won't be able to rely on anything. The memory of your home here will be covered over by darkness as soon as you enter into LIFE."

"So how do I navigate my way through LIFE when you're not there?" Oron asked. He was more confused now than when he started his questions. He was beginning to see that knowledge about LIFE wasn't going to help him get through it. He would simply have to find his way. Ai answered his questions, but he knew the journey was about many things and having answers wasn't going to make it easier.

"There will be stories about me – many stories. And there will be stories of other journeys taken by spirits like you. But darkness will taint the stories and bring confusion. Wars will be fought over the smallest differences. Anger will erupt everywhere in the sanctuary of LIFE, because of disagreement over the details. They will have forgotten that they are connected. And they will follow tainted stories through their entire LIFE like herds of sheep, lost in darkness. Nevertheless, they will learn the mystery. And they will understand darkness."

As with everything Ai created, nothing was wasted and all that transpired for each spirit in the sanctuary would bring about a transformation. For the very idea of loss was a fiction in heaven. Perfect love could never lose. It was impossible. And even the test of darkness in the LIFE sanctuary would demonstrate to the spirits all the more, the incredible power of love.

Oron kept trying to imagine how LIFE would be but darkness was such a foreign idea without meaning. He had no feeling or experience to connect to it. After more consideration and reflection, Oron felt ready.

"There is no way I can know everything about LIFE. I just have to take the journey," he said to himself.

Ai knew his thoughts and smiled. Ai's smile permeated the entire expanse of heaven and created a colorful fragrant breeze that swept instantly over everything. Everyone loved those moments. And he smiled often.

Oron was ready and the time was right for his journey to begin.

"Your first act in LIFE will be to bring pain to another. Bringing intense pain is the only door into LIFE. But it will pass."

As Ai spoke these words he drew his hand over Oron's spirit causing him to lose his sight. Oron was not afraid because the warmth of Ai's presence surrounded him.

Then something happened that Oron would never see. A tear fell from Ai's left eye as he looked upon Oron's face for the last time. It rolled down his cheek and he caught it in his hand. As it dropped it transformed into a brilliant diamond. In silence Ai deposited the diamond into Oron's spirit. Instantly Oron felt himself fall from his celestial home, though it felt more like a dream. Then, like a whisper, he fell into the darkness and was seen in the heavens no more.

3

The Sanctuary

It was difficult to interpret the cries of a newborn. Even after all his needs were met, he continued to cry for no apparent reason. He was so helpless he had no way of telling anyone what upset him so much. The poor little thing would turn red from the anguish. As the days passed, he often cried at night, while his mother agonized over staying away to train him to stop. At first she couldn't take it and had to pick him up to comfort him. But the infant instantly learned that crying brought comfort, so that lesson needed to be unlearned. It was his first lesson in an alien world.

The infant's torment came from the spirit within him, sensing darkness for the first time. The newborn knew nothing. He was a fresh vessel without knowledge of his new world, but also without much control over his body. His spirit was struggling to get free, but could not. He was trapped inside the darkness of LIFE.

The first days in the dark mindless host were the most difficult for the spirit. Unlike his celestial home, where he could move at great speed in any direction, this place was like a dark, damp prison with a strange dull pounding sound like a drum that never stopped – no beautiful vibrations and no colorful lights.

Spirits were made of light, so that was naturally the environment they preferred to live in. They were used to moving freely and with great velocity. They could soar to the highest heights, usually their preference, or descend to the most profound depths. To be limited by something as heavy and sluggish as a body was the worst experience imaginable. It was bondage. And there was no way the spirit could free himself, other than through death. Death was the only way a spirit could sever himself and escape back to his home in the light. Ai knew the spirits would want to leave the minute they were surrounded by complete darkness. That was why he created a bond between the spirit and the host. The host needed to contain the spirit in order to stay alive in the sanctuary, so, when the host felt a spirit enter, he bound himself to the spirit, thus preventing the spirit's escape.

For what spirit with all his capacity would ever choose to endure darkness and pain over freedom and light? Likewise, the host into which he was cast, living in the sanctuary of LIFE, adapted that same urge to be free and search for the light. And throughout the entire journey of LIFE, the spirit was, in fact, gagged and bound by his host, having a mind of its own, which grew very quickly from birth.

Within every host in the sanctuary, the same deep desire persisted because of the longing of his spirit – the need to be free. Although the host couldn't define this desire, it became his strongest instinct deep within. And although the spirit was not seen or heard in the sanctuary, it could never be completely silenced by the host and it's presence was often felt in a gut instinct.

The newborn fussed and cried, and refused to be coddled. How could his mother know that though all his needs were met, the infant was crying because his spirit was feeling so desperate? It felt lost and alone and for the first time was experiencing something new – something called darkness. Being held close to his mother's breast gave the infant comfort sometimes, but the poor spirit just sobbed at the realization that he was trapped. Initially the infant's eyesight was poor, but it was still the only source of light that his frightened little spirit could grasp.

The anxious mother tried to settle her baby, but all this was so new and she was afraid. Then, instinctively she began to sing a lull-a-bye. She surprised herself because it was the first time she'd ever sung the song she remembered her mother singing to her when she was a child. And so the pattern was repeated. The vibration of sound in her voice finally calmed the infant, reminding his spirit of his celestial home.

In reality, the mother's spirit already knew the spirit in the infant. They were kindred spirits in the light. Both knew that the heavens were full of music. The mother responded instinctively, knowing the melodic vibration of her voice would settle the new spirit's fears. The sound of her voice became his first safe place in this strange dark world.

Though the host had a mind of his own, there were moments when the voice of the spirit could be heard which made his light shine a little brighter. Those moments occurred, often when darkness suddenly became too overwhelming, or when a connection was made between spirits. But for most of the journey, LIFE was lived through the mind. Every experience was different, and spirits grew in different ways. The mind of one might grow much stronger than another, and some were more sensitive to their spirits than others.

The reason hosts prayed in desperate moments was because the mind was at a loss to understand. Like the spirit within, it also sought light. And prayer was a way of reaching toward the light – a way to summon hope. Ai loved hearing prayers, not because of their words, but because in those prayers he could hear the voice of the spirits whom he cherished and missed so much.

In the sanctuary of LIFE where darkness ruled, the spirit sought light continuously, even when his own host was oblivious. Of course, the most amazing thing happened when there was a connection between mind and spirit. That was when the host could experience the light of heaven within his spirit. It was always magical and unexpected.

It was a most intriguing LIFE journey for the spirits. Ai had set them on a journey from which they could not escape. And no matter what the experience was, they were bound to grow. Spirits did not all react the same way to darkness. Some constantly tried to escape while others resigned themselves to it and learned to cope. Some could resist fear, while others gave in to it and darkness consumed them.

The host that Ai had designed for the sanctuary of LIFE was remarkable and very different from spirits. Ai gave each host five tools and two reservoirs to use in LIFE. The tools enabled him to interpret, define and live in the sanctuary. He called them the five sensations. Each sensation enabled the host to deposit his interpretations into the two reservoirs. The reservoirs were his mind, which was blank at first and his emotions, which were also empty at infancy. These tools should have served the host well but the sanctuary was ruled by darkness and it tainted the five sensations with a dense fog. This fog caused confusion and fear.

Ai had given a lot of thought to the host's design and although his first idea was to create something more perfect as he tended to do, it occurred to him that the truest test of perfection would be imperfection. Mating the two would ignite that amazing phenomenon called "growth". And Ai loved growth because it was the clear evidence of creation literally creating itself. And it fascinated Ai.

Ai prevented the spirits from entering LIFE exactly as they were in heaven. In heaven, spirits had no gender, or more precisely, they existed with both. It wasn't so much that they were male and female but that they were complete or whole and gender had no meaning in heaven for it did not exist. Upon a spirits entry into LIFE, he would leave behind an essence and so a part of the spirit remained in heaven. This resulted in either a male or female deficiency when a spirit entered his newborn host. Ai prepared for this by making the hosts both male and female. This very deficiency was what drove a host to find a mate. He or she was actually seeking his or her own lost part. And hosts believed they could find their missing self in another. That belief was perpetuated and woven into every culture in the sanctuary. But the division of male and female also ignited countless conflicts for the hosts.

Ai was fascinated by the imperfection of the host. In fact he was thrilled by the inherent effect imperfection could have on perfection in each instance. And LIFE would be a great assimilation of the two. For a perfect spirit would be held by an imperfect host with no escape short of death. Ai already knew the outcome, for he had taken the journey and knew about the struggles of living in the bondage of LIFE. He took the journey so that he, being perfect, would understand the weight of imperfection. It wasn't that he didn't understand imperfection, but rather that he wanted to feel it in every fiber of his being and he wanted to be consumed by darkness so that his light could expand. And it did. For growth was one of the incredible byproducts of creation. It simply emerged from the energy of whatever was created. Ai loved to witness growth in everything. And he was keenly interested to watch his beloved spirits expand in new ways.

While the hosts and the spirits were intertwined together in LIFE, the human host's mind was continually haunted by its own imperfection and constantly tried to attain perfection. In fact the pursuit of perfection would contribute to some of the sanctuary's most fascinating stories, but at the same time to its worst violence. But in everything there was growth, even in destruction. Many imperfections were planted into the host for the sake of expansion.

The baby grew into a strong, healthy child, and with each passing day the anguish of his spirit was soon forgotten. The child became less aware of his spirit and more in touch with the tangible world around him – the one he could experience with his five sensations. The only time when the child became distressed was at night, in the darkness. It was something he couldn't get used to. Darkness made him afraid and reminded his spirit of how he felt when he first came to LIFE. Otherwise, the mind of the host grew quickly and the memory of his spirit's presence faded, overtaken by all the new knowledge of a tangible world – the world of the sanctuary.

So the spirit within him fell asleep and its light dimmed to a faint hue like the glow cast off by the moon on a clear night – a faded residue of the brilliance of heaven. If he had no chance to shine, a spirit would sleep, for shinning was what spirits were made to do. They were beings of light, expressing all the wonders of their brilliant celestial home. At first, it appeared as though there was no purpose for them in the sanctuary at all. LIFE was a world of sensations and the spirit had none of those. It only had light. But although it slept, its glow burned dimly as it remained bound together with the host through his entire journey.

4

Darkness

The host in which Oron's spirit lived was named Uriel. His Portuguese mother had given him that name because she was impressed by a story she'd heard about a man from Portugal named Uriel da Costa. He was a devout man who fought desperately for religious truth. He was seeking the light, and in doing so he tried to expose darkness. In the end he was defeated and humiliated and took his own life. His death was a victory for darkness, but it inspired others who would take up his cause. Uriel's mother believed in heaven as it was taught to her in childhood. She prayed often although she wasn't certain her prayers were heard.

Young Uriel had no knowledge of the darkness, other than physical darkness at night, which still frightened him. But the invisible darkness in the sanctuary was so pervasive it could settle into every aspect of LIFE without detection. Hosts grew so accustomed to living in darkness they hardly noticed, even though all of them had struggled with it in the beginning. In the sanctuary, darkness was a part of LIFE. It persistently tried to creep into the two reservoirs of the host. It clouded his understanding and just as light brought peace and harmony to spirits in the heavens, darkness flooded the sanctuary with fear, suspicion and strife. One of the most insidious things about darkness was its ability to prevent a host from finding his true self. Its goal was to keep the host from realizing the true power he possessed in the form of a perfect spirit living right there inside him. If successful then the spirit's light would never be able to expose the paralyzing control of darkness over the host and his journey. Hosts were hesitant to believe in their own light because they were conditioned to living in a world experienced through sensations. And that was all they knew. Darkness convinced them that the stories in their reservoirs were the only truth. And hosts became driven mostly by their emotions, which were filled with so many random thoughts. Many hosts believed that every thought or idea needed to be verified by the five sensations otherwise it could not true. And those who reached for understanding beyond the senses embarked on a path of uncertainty, and often returned to living within their sensations. Darkness had presided in the sanctuary for so long that for most, the five sensations offered the only truth that could be trusted. So they were kept from seeking their own inner light. And yet the light was right there all along – so close yet completely unseen. Ultimately, many who lived in the sanctuary learned to be suspicious of the idea of heaven and even questioned its very existence.

The only reason that invisible darkness was so powerful in the sanctuary was because of the absence of invisible light. A spirit living in a host was suppressed by the host's mind and therefore kept isolated and unable to offer any effective guidance. Ironically, everyone knew they possessed their own spirit, but they didn't understand its value other than as an entity existing in every person. So the spirit remained in a dormant state, but not an unconscious sleep. It was a sleep in which the spirit was aware of everything, but powerless to guide and so, remained silent.

Uriel grew into a robust young man. But similar to the tragic hero of his namesake, Uriel was searching. His mind was sharp and active – full of stories and commentaries, but in spite of all he'd learned, he was left with more questions than answers. Uriel had no idea that he, like every other host, was carrying perfection inside and its light held the answers to all his questions.

Stories were very important in the sanctuary of LIFE and hosts everywhere created their reality, their culture and their entire existence around them.

In heaven, Ai knew about the stories. He knew the value placed on them in LIFE, but he also knew how stories became used as weapons. It troubled him that stories, about him in particular, resulted in causing so much hatred and war, no matter how miraculous the stories were originally. Darkness tainted every story, which caused suspicion in every culture of the sanctuary. Many believed their version, whatever it was, was the only truth. And their beliefs led them to form enemies of others. Everyone wanted to be right, because they thought it gave them power. But Ai knew stories couldn't give anyone power. The only real power was within each of them. It was held inside the only piece of heaven they possessed in LIFE – their spirits. But because their spirits couldn't be verified by the five sensations, they could not believe. So they searched outwardly for answers in every other direction – always searching, never finding.

As he grew, Uriel's unanswered questions only led him to despair. He clung to LIFE instinctively but at the same time wanted to escape. Learning came easily to him, but he found himself unable to focus on one idea for very long. It was difficult for him to relax. His mind was like a dog chasing its tail endlessly – never ceasing, to the point of exhaustion. Mental exhaustion always threw him into deep frustration. And still the questions taunted him – still unanswered.

His mother raised Uriel. His father was often away on business, and just before his tenth birthday, his mother informed him that his father would not be coming home at all anymore. He never forgot the day she told him. He remembered everything about that day, even the clothes he was wearing. She was in the kitchen doing dishes, wearing her apron. After announcing the news, she slumped into a chair, without even looking up. She seemed to be looking into the past as she talked about his father not coming home. Uriel remembered watching the tears streaming down his mother's face. It was the first time he'd ever seen her cry. Words could not describe what he was feeling at that moment, and he hated it. There in front of him sat the personification of strength: the one who fed him, clothed him and calmed all his fears. She was the comfort for his every need and the answer to every childhood question. And there she was, crushed and sobbing like a helpless child. How could that be when he was the child? She'd been his pillar of strength and now she was broken. It was wrong but there was nothing he could do to fix it. He wasn't even sure what to feel.

At that precise moment, something within Uriel changed forever. It felt like his heart was going to burst with sadness. Perhaps it did, for the pain he felt pierced his heart like a knife and wounded him deeply. That wound would change his character. And it buried itself in his spirit.

He reached out his hand to wipe the tears from her face and said, "Don't worry, mama. I will take care of you." The instant he reached out to touch her face he felt the strangest sensation. It was as though he'd already seen this exact moment in time. In fact, he had. It was his spirit's first pearl from the BOOK OF LIFE. And that pearl would dig the wound that was forming in his spirit. From that moment on, Uriel knew he must be strong. He felt as though he'd been given a mission to protect his mother from pain, for up to this point, she'd been the center of his world. He vowed never to abandon her.

This was the first of many pearls Uriel would experience in LIFE. They were pearls of great value for they had the power to touch his spirit and give it a voice. Although Uriel had no knowledge of heaven, the first image his spirit chose had already occurred. In heaven, Ai had promised Oron that the pearl would carve a hole into his spirit. And it did.

As Uriel grew, he was hungry for knowledge and had a passion for reading books on every subject. His latent desire for answers led him to a preoccupation with acquiring knowledge, which was considered an admirable pursuit in LIFE. Those who sought to gain knowledge were respected and the acquisition of stories was a highly esteemed pursuit in the sanctuary. Those with the greatest collection of stories were able to carry the greatest influence over others and had the freedom to perpetuate stories of their own. Within the parameters of the five sensations, it was wise to learn as much as one could about LIFE in the sanctuary. Uriel's pursuit for knowledge allowed him to excel in his world.

His questions led him to study the one thing that intrigued him most and something over which he had the least control – his mind. He was so well versed in the mind that he came to believe that little else was real other than what existed in the mind. He believed the mind was responsible for all reality and that perception was a reflection of one's state of mind, whatever it was. If the mind were healthy, perception and actions would be healthy. If the mind were sick, then perception would also be twisted. In his mind, there was nothing beyond the sanctuary and the highest achievement one could hope for was to fill the mind with all knowledge. That was what Uriel, in all his seeking, had come to believe. But in spite of his thoughts and opinions, which were expressed confidently, Uriel was secretly haunted by the unanswered questions. And as his knowledge increased, so also, did his questions.

Ai looked upon Uriel with great compassion. It was time. The diamond deposited into Oron's spirit on his descent into LIFE contained something innate and eternal – Ai's essence. And with it, Ai could be a part of Oron's adventure through

LIFE. Being there, albeit undetected by Uriel, was essential to Ai.

With all his knowledge, Uriel still remained blind to what was within his spirit. But it was time for Uriel to have a glimpse. It would not be easy and he would not be open to it at first, but the diamond pulsated within his spirit, and finally Uriel would begin to understand its mystery.

5

Awakening

Diamonds were reflections of heaven. Everything that refracted light giving the appearance of movement offered a reflection of heaven's light. Although hosts didn't understand why, they greatly valued stones that sparkled calling them "precious". How could they know as they gazed upon precious stones that their spirits within were glowing with thoughts of their forgotten celestial home? Not only were hosts inspired by shinning stones, but also by lakes and oceans that glittered under the sun, and snowflakes or waterfalls that sparkled in the sunlight, or the moonlight. Any form of light captured attention in the sanctuary. That residue of heaven lived in every host. And whether it was from the warm glow of a burning candle or the brilliant sun on the brightest day, the reminders could not be ignored and carried a comforting sense of security. Some called it peace. It was like a fresh breeze, sweeping through their minds giving them the most wonderful sensation of hope – such was the effect of natural light in the sanctuary. Whether long or short, that moment always had the same effect – and with it a sense of freedom. And the host's spirit instinctively glowed in response to the light he witnessed and the moment was magical. When Ai created the sanctuary he knew that filling it with such reflectors was important. Those images of light would always be a great comfort in LIFE. Reflectors were all the ways light could penetrate through darkness and be experienced by the hosts. They could be created by any impression of light in the sanctuary. The sun was an effective tool for exposing reflectors. Although relatively dim itself, the sun was more than brilliant enough for the sanctuary.

Uriel held a position as a teacher, for his knowledge was valuable. He'd learned a great number of stories and also knew what countless other hosts had concluded about LIFE in the sanctuary. That was important to the hosts. Opinions carried a lot of weight. This was odd because opinions didn't even need to be true or accurate. Uriel could quote entire collections of opinions and thoughts from others who had lived in the sanctuary long before him.

Ai was intrigued by LIFE in the sanctuary and how it took on its own reality without him. He saw how quickly the hosts learned all they could through their sensations and how they rewarded themselves for this knowledge. It was almost like a game they played. And although they pursued knowledge, they knew nothing about the incredible power that slept inside each one of them. It was a power that moved beyond the parameters of all knowledge – a power that could propel them beyond their imagination. But it slept.

In his continuous search for knowledge, Uriel came across a small bit of information about a peculiar man who was said to live in a small town in a remote part of the sanctuary. It was reported by several accounts that this particular man possessed confounding wisdom. It was true that some who lived in the sanctuary were more aware of their spirituality than others and they often lived in remote areas. But they were hard to find. These particular hosts were referred to as sages because their awareness gave them a deeper knowledge about LIFE beyond the sanctuary.

Uriel was intrigued by the possibility of gaining new insight. Perhaps it would fill the dark void he felt inside.

Darkness was like an indefinable emptiness – a disconnectedness, always lurking in his mind. And so, his imagination ran wild about what he might learn from this sage.

One of the consequences of that common feeling of discontentment among hosts brought about the culture of the dream-weavers. They were those with an appetite for power. It was like their drug. They too were blinded by darkness, but the dream-weavers claimed to have 'the light'. Their intent was to capitalize on hope – a commodity desperately sought after by the hosts. There were many kinds of dream-weavers throughout the many cultures of the sanctuary, and although their differences were vast, they always made the same claim – to have the one great hope.

In reality, it was impossible for any one of them to have the one great hope but they were skillfully able to persuade hosts with clever stories. Some were so skilled they prospered greatly and were given immense power. The most effective tool used whenever new members were gained was ironically the same tool used by darkness – it was fear. And because stories were so loved in the sanctuary, dream-weavers created elaborate ones promising all kinds of rewards for allegiance and a horrible end for those who refused to comply. It was all about using fear to control and it worked beautifully. The weak and lonely, who felt lost in the sanctuary, fell prey to the dream-weavers simply because they wanted to belong somewhere. They were captivated by elaborate stories about a perfect life filled with everything that glittered and glowed.

And so darkness played along and was delighted by the dream-weaver's game. It cleverly kept the hosts blind to their own true light – which was to be their guide through the darkness.

Sages were sought after by dream-weavers because the hosts were naturally intrigued by real sages. So the dream-weavers sought to employ the services of a sage in their cause.

They knew the value in having a sage as their figurehead in that it would add to their credibility and power. But in reality, true sages had no interest in the game. They lived in solitude without revealing themselves. They were only interested in truth and considered the dream-weaver's game to be complete nonsense. True sages had the wisdom to see through the error in making a business out of desperation so they removed themselves from view.

Although everyone knew about dream-weavers, some were wary of them and stayed away, while others, feeling lost, found their way into the game. Those who played were easily identified by those who did not, because they often chose to separate themselves. And sadly, those who played the game became blinded by it. They believed that being part of the game gave them more value than those on the "outside". Perhaps it was because they belonged to something, while others did not. Pride inevitably settled upon their minds like a fog and they were unable to think beyond the stories created by their dream-weavers. Many became so involved in their particular game that they gave up complete control of their minds and were like robots, willing to obey anything they were told. Ai was disappointed when that happened because those spirits didn't have a chance to find their true selves within the journey and experience the mystery of LIFE in the sanctuary.

Every culture and generation had its own brand of dream-weavers and many of them were so successful at the game that they could pass it down for many generations before it lost its power.

Ai knew that as long as there were those who felt lost, there would always be a place for new dream-weavers and their new games. Every spirit had once known the connectedness in the great expanse of heaven, and that feeling also touched the mind of every host in the sanctuary. Being without it left a host feeling a sense of loss. And the game was there to offer a sense of belonging. It was a comfort few could resist. No wonder the dream-weavers became so strong. Once caught, it was very difficult for a host to free himself from the game.

☼

Uriel uncovered what he could about the location of the alleged sage and decided to search him out. He had no idea whether the sage really existed. He just knew he had to at least attempt to find him. The sage was said to be living near a town in the northern hemisphere. It was a remote place with few inhabitants. That was due to the harsh climate.

On a bright sunny day, Uriel boarded a small plane heading north. He felt as if the weather on such a beautiful day was silently applauding his decision to take the trip. It was something he'd wanted to do for a long time, even though he never imagined this could be happening. In fact, he had no idea six months earlier that he would be taking such a random trip up north. But Uriel also had no idea that it would mark the beginning of a journey to change his life forever.

6

The North

The cold northern peaks stood silently, like ancient kings sleeping in their majestic thrones for all eternity. They gave the impression of holding timeless secrets, and yet they were no more than icy masses of stone, coated in a blanket of white. The peaks held no regard for LIFE in the sanctuary, nor did they answer to anyone. But travelers were captivated by their beauty and inspired by their grandeur. Perhaps it was because the towering, icy peaks were reaching toward the heavens, and their impression quickened all who gazed upon them with a reminder of home – another reflector.

Far below, a small town nestled tightly into the frozen valley. The town had once been a hub of activity in earlier times when prospectors came there to seek their fortunes. Now it was quiet and sparsely populated. If a sage lived there, it should be easy to find him, for in severe climates such as this the hosts tended to be familiar with everyone and knew most everything about each other's activities.

The main street consisted of a handful of buildings huddled together – as if to keep warm. The first place Uriel stopped was at the main street tavern. He thought it might be the best place to learn about a sage. He knew it would be the one place in town where all the best stories were told – true or not.

Upon entering the tavern, Uriel spotted several empty stools at one end of the bar. People pretended not to notice him, but they were very aware of his presence. It wasn't often a stranger entered, and when one did, it was a curiosity to the locals.

The bartender, also the owner, felt the weight of his role in the town. His skill was serving drinks. He knew everyone and proudly served up the cure to all their troubles in the form of whatever drink they wanted. Upon seeing Uriel at the door, the bartender already identified his brand of trouble. He astutely surmised that the stranger was looking for someone and pretended not to notice Uriel sit down. Then, as was his style, he spoke to Uriel without looking up.

"A rough flight in?" he asked. Uriel looked around to see if anyone else was within earshot. Realizing the man was addressing him he answered,

"More than I'm used to."

"Always is," he looked over. "What's your poison?"

Bartenders seemed to possess a carnal wisdom about the world – perhaps from all stories they'd heard. Uriel didn't quite know how to ask his question. Would this bartender think him crazy for coming right out and asking if he knew of a sage living outside of town?

"Whatever you have on tap is fine." Uriel hesitated, not wanting to appear too anxious. He looked around for a few minutes before continuing.

"Hey listen, I'm doing some research."

That was a good one whether it was true or not. The bar owner knew it meant anything. Usually it meant running away from something or someone. The only other type of visitor didn't normally travel alone – either a film crew or a research team.

"Oh yeah?" he pretended to be uninterested.

"What would you say is the population of this town?"

"Under two thousand."

"So you know just about everyone." Uriel laughed. The bartender didn't crack a smile. It was an unspoken code not to smile easily.

"Who you lookin' for?"

Uriel was stumped. It was a simple enough question. Getting information without drawing attention wasn't going to be easy. How could he put it without sounding strange?

"Kind of a... sage," he blurted. Not the subtlety he intended. The bartender turned around and walked over to Uriel. He stared at him as though he were trying to read his thoughts.

Darkness reigned in every part of the sanctuary. No matter how remote or beautiful the scenery, darkness was king. And though it didn't reveal itself to the eyes, every human spirit sensed its presence. Darkness was like a ravenous animal, always hungry, always hunting. But its prey was hope, truth and most of all light. And those who sought after these kinds of treasures needed to be persistent. Everyone who lived in the darkness of the sanctuary was susceptible to its toxins – of which fear and suspicion were a few.

"There's no 'wise man' in these parts, mister, unless you're talkin' about crazy old Aquilo up on Mystic Ridge. And you'd have a hell of a time getting there now", replied the bartender.

At that moment he decided he didn't like the stranger – even if it was for the simple fact that his question was unusual and suspicious.

Darkness was approaching and daylight was quickly fading. Uriel decided to wait till morning to look for this 'crazy old Aquilo '.

At the first sign of light, Uriel enquired around town about the old man and found himself slowly gathering bits and pieces of potentially useful information as to his whereabouts. He had no idea if this Aquilo was a sage or just a crazy old man. Age wasn't indicative of wisdom and Uriel knew that he could well be wasting his time. If not for his characteristic curiosity, he would have certainly turned around by now.

By mid morning, Uriel was already on the path heading to Mystic Ridge. He'd rented a snowmobile with specific instructions to where he was going. He had hoped to hire a guide, but no one was available to take him. At least that's what he was told. The trip should have taken him about an hour, but somewhere along the way he missed one of the markers, which wasn't difficult to do considering it had started to snow heavily and he couldn't see two feet in front of him.

After two hours, Uriel decided to stop and wait for the snow to let up. He didn't want to run out of gas. He found shelter under a few trees and sat there covered by an old woolen blanket on his snowmobile and waited. Several hours passed and still the snow fell heavy. Uriel started to feel a bit cold. Unaware of the danger, he began to feel drowsy and fell asleep.

Darkness moved in, and with it, death crept along the ground toward Uriel. The sanctuary could be a cold place with no mercy for the weak and Uriel, in his sleep, was becoming weaker by the minute. With darkness approaching and the hope of Uriel's quest fading quickly, his spirit, Oron suddenly let out a burst of light. These moments were not so rare in the sanctuary but they were seldom seen or recognized. Oron's burst of light rushed straight to Ai and could be detected by a sudden twinkle in his eye, if anyone had been watching. Ai stopped what he was doing, looked toward the sanctuary and blew. A warm breeze brushed through the heavens, as it often did. Only this one was for Oron.

A pot was bubbling over the fire. Aquilo liked to cook his soup this way, even though he had a perfectly good stove in the kitchen. He stared at the fire, mesmerized by its glowing light, and just at that moment there was a twinkle in his eye. Of course nobody else was there to see it. As if he'd just had an epiphany, Aquilo got up and threw his coat on. He went back to the fire to remove the pot. Then he took out a spoon and had a taste, something he entitled himself to if he was going out in the nasty weather. He took his flashlight, a knapsack, and a few old bear hides and went out to tie up his dog team. In minutes he was away, flying through the sea of snowflakes like a crazy old wizard. He had no idea where he was going and strangely enough, that was of no concern to him.

The fire raged in its bed and warmth filled the room. Its heat flushed over Uriel's face and he awoke. When he opened his eyes, Uriel looked straight at the fire. He didn't move. At that moment he felt safe and warm. In fact, he felt more completely at home than he'd felt in a very long time, which was strange because he had no idea where he was. As he watched the fire, a smiling old face came into view.

"Thought you were dead," said the old man with a chuckle and a wink. Suddenly Uriel realized how stupid he'd been. Why on earth would he follow a whim like that? Underestimating the elements was just pure stupidity. He was embarrassed. He should have known better. After all, he was a man well respected for his knowledge about many things in LIFE. And here he was on an escapade to some strange place with what now seemed like little more than a child's fantasy guiding him. Ridiculous!

And yet, it felt like he was in a dream. Perhaps he was dead, he thought to himself, and this old man was God or something. God was the name those in his culture used to describe an all powerful force that they thought might have created the sanctuary. Similar to Ai, except most of the time the hosts depicted this God to look and act like them, which greatly darkened him and negated his light. Although notions about him were varied from one extreme to another, many hosts seemed to have a dim inkling of him and perceived him to be 'out there' somewhere.

"Welcome back, son", said the old man moving out of Uriel's line of sight. Uriel knew that he should have felt uncomfortable but strangely he was not. He was unusually relaxed. Something about the place made him feel serene. He sat up slowly, and looked around the room. It was a simple log cabin, as one would expect. Everything extended out from the hearth, which was the life pulse of the home. It was virtually one big room with a bed in the corner and a kitchen area on the other side. The old man returned with a big bowl of soup and placed it on a little table beside Uriel.

"This will warm your bones." He said.

"Thank you." Uriel was overwhelmed by the old man's sense of jolliness. His personality had as much warmth as did his cabin. "How did you find me?"

"I knew you were lost and in trouble."

The old man had discernment. Uriel felt his heart jump. The old man sounded wise. Could he really be a sage? Just the thought of it caused his emotions to well up inside him. It was a raw feeling and he couldn't help himself. A lifetime of emotions wanted to break free but he was afraid of embarrassing himself. And at the same time he felt such an intense desire to let himself go. He could feel himself beginning to crumble inside but forced himself to stay composed. What was all this emotion? He felt the way a troubled child feels who acts tough around strangers, but upon seeing his mother as a safe place, breaks down and shows his true feelings. Uriel might have found a sage, and in that, the hope of finding answers for a lifetime of nagging questions. It was a discovery he could hardly contain.

The old man sensed Uriel's turmoil and knew he was experiencing a slight meltdown. It was as much a thawing of his mind as it was for his body by the warmth of the hearth. "Eat now", he said quietly and went outside to feed the dogs, giving Uriel time alone to adjust and settle his thoughts and emotions.

Uriel sat awhile longer staring at the blazing fire, thinking about all the things that had led him to this place. His thoughts followed a logical sequence, as they always did, and he reviewed in his mind how events had directed his path. He always thought the events were random, but now that he was here in this lost cabin, in a frozen landscape, he was trying to connect the events like a child connects dots to uncover a hidden picture.

He drank the soup and its taste reminded him of his childhood. His thoughts took him to the day he came into the room and saw his mother crying. That event deeply impacted him. On one hand he had resolved to save his mother from any further pain, but the event also frightened him. He wondered if he, like his father, had the same tendency to be unable to maintain a marriage and family. Obviously his father wasn't and in spite of how Uriel resented his father for leaving, he was afraid that he might do the same. This fear prevented Uriel from forming deep ties to a woman. His relationships had always been more superficial and the thought of marriage was something that had always made him feel very uncomfortable.

The wind blew in a waft of snow before Aquilo could close the cabin door behind him. His arms were laden with firewood as he used his foot to push the door shut. He approached the hearth, glancing down at his houseguest. He set down the wood and turned to study the stranger's face. He sensed the man's turmoil but beyond that he felt the man's spirit calling out to him. The old man could see beyond the five sensations. He was seeing with his spirit – something he'd learned to do in the wilderness. There was a point at which death would have overtaken him had he not learned to let his spirit guide him, especially in the harsh and unforgiving climate of the north. He too had once been a young man searching for answers. But answers were a strange thing. Those who claimed to seek them didn't realize what they were asking for and were often unable to accept them. Aquilo, unlike most, had persevered beyond the answers. For answers, in themselves, were not truth, but only signposts to the truth and many could not sustain the journey to the point of truth.

Aquilo felt his spirit shimmer. It had been a long winter in the north. The time had come to share his path. It was long anticipated.

The storm subsided as quickly as it had appeared. As the skies cleared, the heavens danced with a billion stars and other amazing lights that could only be seen in these parts. But the glory of the heavens danced in a private performance for an audience that was already asleep.

The morning sun cast a warm glow on the frozen white peaks. Mountains saluted the dawn with majestic pride and indifference, their rugged beauty enhanced by the light of the sun. Aquilo was preparing for an excursion. Uriel awoke from his peaceful slumber feeling completely renewed. He ventured outside to find the old man harnessing his dogs to a sled. The old man seemed young, moving with a spring in his step. Uriel didn't have a chance to ask anything. After taking a minute to introduce himself he said,

"Grab the extra supplies on the table while I tie the dogs. We're going on an excursion and we have to make good time to be back before dark. And get yourself some breakfast while you're in there." There were warm buns on the stove and coffee in an old tin pot. Uriel was excited and the bread and coffee tasted unusually good with the thought of an impending adventure to follow.

In no time they were off and Uriel was amazed how easily the dogs pulled them through the snow. He'd seen it many times but never felt the actual sensation of being pulled by a dog team. He understood why this was so much better than a machine. There was a sense of connectedness and symmetry in a world of man and beast sharing the journey. After a few hours the terrain became rugged and the dogs slowed their pace. In this white wilderness Uriel was impressed by how the old man seemed to be able to navigate his way through the snow, easily finding the most accessible routes. He seemed to know the way well, as though he'd traveled it a thousand times. The truth was the old man had only been here a few times before and his navigation skills were far less used than Uriel knew. But Aquilo traveled with another navigation tool. One that Uriel wasn't aware of yet.

They traveled over hills and ridges, neither one speaking, both lost in thought. Then Aquilo stopped the dogs in front of a rock face that appeared to be hollowed out on one side. He stepped off the sled and looked back at Uriel, saying nothing. Uriel took it as a sign to follow. Aquilo walked away expecting as much. He stepped into the hollow of the rock and crouched down to pass under a jagged edge that dipped down like a short curtain at the opening. The stone curtain was a natural formation in the rock, but it seemed to be there intentionally perhaps to conceal the entryway – as if nature itself did not want anyone to notice its secret door.

Aquilo shot back a look at Uriel but said nothing. It was the look a parent gives a son, when he is about to venture out on his own. It was a look that said, 'This is serious, pay attention.' Aquilo continued and the hollow turned into a narrow tunnel for a few feet. Then, as if walking into a dark cathedral with light pouring in though the windows washing over its beauty, they stepped into the most beautiful sun drenched cathedral of ice. It was unlike anything Uriel could imagine. There was a great opening up above and an underground waterfall, part of which was frozen. The mist from the water had settled over time into the most intricate and delicate icicles that looked more like crystal snowflakes in appearance but much larger in size. The sunlight, pouring in from above, reflected the light everywhere and gave the illusion of diamonds. The light was refracted by countless crystals of ice creating prisms of colors dancing all over the walls. It was a magnificent work of art created by nature and untouched by human hands – a cathedral of light. Uriel was frozen. The immense beauty had captivated him and he stood completely still. They both felt the glory of such incredible beauty touch them right to the core. Their spirits danced. Uriel was exhilarated. Unimaginable beauty had ignited him and he could feel its effects pulsating through his entire body. Without looking at him, Aquilo spoke,

"You have come here to find answers but you have not asked the right questions. This is because your mind has blinded you. You're proud of all that you know, and yet, you do not know your true self."

Oh yes, the questions. He'd completely forgotten about them. Everything paled in comparison to the frozen paradise surrounding him at that moment. Aquilo continued.

"First I'll tell you who you are and then you'll know the only question you need to ask." Aquilo studied the beautiful ice crystals, each one uniquely formed over time by the cold mist from the waterfall and he continued,

"What you see around you is magnificent. But it's only a dim shadow of the place where you're from. Your spirit is awakened by this beauty, because in it you've been reminded of your true home. But your true self which is hidden inside you, is unseen and forgotten. That's why you're a stranger to yourself and you feel confused. It's the work of darkness. You were closer to the truth when you knew nothing at birth. But darkness slowly poisoned your mind and thus kept you from seeing your true self."

Uriel wondered how Aquilo could be so sure of all this but he was reluctant to interrupt the old man for fear that he might stop talking. And he didn't want him to stop. It was as if the words were feeding him in some strange way and Uriel had to hear more. He focused on the ice crystals and became more aware of the constant roar of the waterfall. It was so bright and beautiful. Framed by the steep rock walls, the waterfall sounded so much louder than it was.

"The day we were born was the day we got lost." Aquilo added.

"So how did you find yourself?" Uriel interrupted. He couldn't help it. He was curious about the old man.

"I always knew I was lost. But the only way to find myself was to remove every illusion. And I came here to this end of the earth – a place lost to the world. And this is where I found myself. Over time my true self began to unfold before me – only as much as I allowed it to."

Uriel barely understood what the old man was talking about but he had a sense that something inside him was hanging on every word.

"Is it time alone that's required to know oneself?" Uriel wanted to understand.

Aquilo's expression grew serious and he stared straight into Uriel's eyes.

"These magnificent crystals are created in complete solitude. No one sees them, yet they continue to grow in beauty and brilliance. They are like our spirits. We have within us the most amazing creative power on earth. Our spirits have created, in another dimension, such magnificence as you see here, and far more than this. Our spirits know all things because they are infinite and perfect. But here on earth they're trapped inside a weak vessel, bound and limited by sensations and thoughts. Our spirits are connected to us and their resources are endless because they are connected to infinity and to each other. And miracles are simply moments when we catch a glimpse of this incredible reality and yet we live with no idea about our true potential." He looked at the ice crystals and continued,

"You're never alone. You only think you are because you have not lived beyond the five sensations. You have not lived by the spirit hidden within you."

"Is that how you live?" Uriel asked.

"I found you because my spirit showed me exactly where you were, just as I found this place."

"How can I live like that?"

Aquilo focused again on Uriel. Then he laughed for the first time since they had arrived. His spirit was energized by the chance to pass on his knowledge to an eager listener. "There's a lot for you to learn and you can't learn it all from me. Now look at the shimmering ice crystals and as you examine each one carefully tell yourself this first truth: THE LIGHT IS WITHIN ME. IT IS THERE TO GUIDE ME AND SHOW ME MY TRUE SELF. IF I SO CHOOSE, MY LIGHT WILL OVERCOME ALL DARKNESS FOR IT TRULY HAS THE POWER TO CREATE IN ME MORE THAN I CAN IMAGINE.

As you say this to yourself, the darkness that has ruled your thoughts will begin to disperse, just as pure oxygen flushes out all the impurities that form in its absence. Then you can allow light to flood deeper into your mind. Do this continually. And from now on, whenever you close your eyes you must imagine this cathedral of light, so take in everything you see right now. Focus on it. Breathe it in. And it will give you peace because it will remind you of the light within you."

Aquilo continued to talk to Uriel, constantly reminding him to focus on the beauty of the crystals with the sound of the waterfall around them. Uriel felt as though he'd stumbled upon an endless moment in which time had ceased to exist. Then Aquilo spoke to him about his spirit and his own personal light.

"The spirit within you bears a name like your own, but different. Your spirit contains the creative power of the entire universe. It came from light and knows only light. It has hidden inside you since just before you were born. Although you carry this light, darkness has deluded you and drawn you into its confines. Darkness is not your companion. It only seeks to consume your light, and it wants you to believe you are powerless and invisible. But it cannot overcome your spirit because your spirit is light. And nothing can destroy light, but only cover it." Aquilo paused for a moment and stepped closer to Uriel. He lowered his voice, speaking in a whisper. His words seemed to be gliding over the waterfall itself.

"So...what is the only question you need to ask?"

Uriel felt the words fall out of his own mouth without really knowing where they came from. The truth was, it was Oron, his spirit, who gave him the words,

"If I am truly made from light and my spirit IS my true self then the only question I must find the answer to is.... how to be human?"

At that instant, a world away, Ai hovered by the crest of vapors. He smiled as a father would smile at his son, who just discovered a new use for an old toy. Oron was emerging and Uriel was beginning to see his true self. Like a flower opens up to the morning sun, the petals of Uriel's life would begin to unfold. It was a beautiful sight and one that only Ai could see from the lofty heights. Aquilo, whose spirit was called Makan, had taken Uriel through the first step. And the revelation of light in his life would finally be given the freedom to grow.

7

A Dark Pause

Driving on the back of a loud cold machine made Uriel feel as though his time with Aquilo was more like a dream than a reality. Darkness was trying to creep into his thoughts. It was filling his mind with doubt and disbelief. How could all this be true? Could there be a reality that functioned so fluidly beyond the world of sensations? And even if it were real, would it change his life so much? The farther he drove away, the more the enchantment of the crystal cave began to fade.

That night Uriel lay in his hotel bed, overwhelmed by doubt. His thoughts were racing. When he finally closed his eyes, he saw a vision of the cave and its brilliant ice crystals. He could hear Aquilo's voice telling him to make a mental picture of it. It was true. He had seen the magnificence of the frozen crystals and as he held that picture in his mind he remembered Aquilo's words and repeated them. And as he did, the darkness lifted, leaving him feeling better and his excitement returned.

He thought about the trip back to the cabin with Aquilo and all the things the old man told him. He could see Aquilo's weathered face and the calm expression in his steely grey eyes. His old face was undeniably familiar – the kind of familiarity that a person felt seeing a distant relative whose face he had always known. That image comforted Uriel. He perceived Aquilo the way a young child perceives a grand father, as a wise gentle giant with wisdom beyond words. Aquilo spoke in riddles, as some grandfathers do, that were just at the edge of Uriel's understanding. He liked the challenge of recalibrating his mind with fresh ideas. It stimulated him. When they were parting ways, he remembered Aquilo saying,

"Truth lies under the illusion, but illusions run deep. It takes persistence to find the truth, but like a buried treasure that inspires you to search, it is well worth the effort. You must be willing to travel far and wide to find it. Take this map. It will show you where to start and along the way you'll learn more about the path upon which you have embarked."

As Uriel mulled over his words he took out the bundled 'map' he'd been given. It was in a pouch, wrapped several times in a cloth. He unwrapped the cloth carefully and pulled out the pouch. Inside was a beautiful crystal, shaped like a blunt icicle with the sides cut into straight edges like an octagon. He'd looked at it when he first returned to the hotel, but could make no sense of it. It reminded him of the crystal cave. Inside the stone was what looked like a pinkish line or crack embedded in the centre of the crystal. It rose and fell across the length of the stone. Along the bottom of the crack there were tiny red flecks. They looked like grains of sand. It could have been gold dust, but the grains were too reddish to be real gold.

Uriel turned it slowly around under the dim light by his bed. It was fascinating but probably not particularly valuable. He couldn't see how this stone would show him anything. He was as confused as he was fascinated by it. Nevertheless it was a constant reminder of the incredible hidden beauty he'd seen in the north.

Oron, his spirit, was fully aware of the crystal. But it wasn't the crystal that made him so excited for the first time in a very long time. It was that he would finally be of more use to his host than just enabling his body to live. Oron longed to expand and create as he had done so freely before he entered this LIFE. He longed to share his infinite light with Uriel and it seemed as if Uriel was finally starting to let go of the idea that he had to be bound by his mind and his sensations. Perhaps Uriel would allow Oron to have a voice, just as he'd given a voice to his own mind.

For as much as Uriel's mind could store information, imprint habits and responses, it could not give Uriel the deep truth about his identity. The true nature of Uriel's identity lay hidden in his spirit. And like a buried treasure, his spirit remained within him, for his entire life thus far, undiscovered. His habits and behavior patterns certainly gave an exterior portrait of Uriel, the 'person', but his inner self was where his true self could be found. It was neither replaceable, nor erasable and would always be of infinite value in the universe, in spite of wherever LIFE in the sanctuary would take him.

In heaven, whenever spirits passed each other, they would spontaneously imbue one another with light and energy, and so the spirits were always being enriched and strengthened by each other. It was impossible to feel invisible because they all engaged in this energizing interaction. That's why Oron had laughed in disbelief at Ai's description of how the effect of darkness could make one feel invisible. But in the sanctuary of LIFE, where spirits were hidden, darkness tainted the minds of the hosts and so the bonds between them were weak at best. In some cases only hostility existed between them and their spirits were unable to recognize each other.

In his own LIFE journey, Ai taught the hosts about was the value of their connectedness with one another. Knowing how important stories were to the hosts, Ai used them a lot to get his point across. With stories, he tried to illustrate how things were different in heaven where spirits were free. One different thing about Ai's journey was that while living in the sanctuary, he hadn't forgotten his home in heaven. So it was difficult to overcome their blindness, but Ai knew his journey was important as a demonstration. He taught the idea of connectedness in stories about caring for each other as neighbors – whether they knew them or not. This was difficult for them to understand because fear taught them not to trust anyone. And though his words lived on in many traditions, darkness always stirred up fear and mistrust, which threatened any bonds they formed.

The only way to show them how to overcome darkness was to teach about the light that was already theirs. But it was a truth they couldn't seem to grasp, for whenever a new idea emerged in the sanctuary, it wasn't long before the light was overcome by darkness as it settled into their minds and darkened their thoughts. Darkness knew how to blind the hosts, which always brought separation. This was the way of darkness, time after time. It made good use of fear, suspicion, greed and even pride. Those were the most effective tools.

Ai never intended the journey of LIFE to be without obstacles. There could be no growth in that. He wanted an environment where the light would have to break through darkness in order to expand itself, and for that to happen, darkness had to be relentless – like a ravenous beast with no mercy. And it was.

☀

Uriel's flight home was uneventful. The farther he was from Aquilo's north, the more it felt like an illusion. Except for the pouch in his pocket and the image in his mind, whenever he closed his eyes, the entire adventure could have been a dream. How quickly the glories of a day could vanish and be forgotten! How forgetful the hosts could be with only a bit of time and distance between them and an infinitely beautiful moment, and how effectively darkness guarded its territory!

Upon his return, Uriel found an abundance of unfinished things needing his attention. At first he told himself he would get things done and refocus on this new path. Every night he picked up the crystal and imagined where it might take him and what the next part of the adventure might be like. But after awhile he stopped taking out the stone and it sat on his night table, wrapped neatly in a cloth tucked inside the pouch, just as his own spirit remained tucked inside his heart, wrapped in the cloth of time lost.

A short time after his return, Uriel had the unexpected pleasure of receiving an award for some of his research, and along with the accolades came new invitations to lecture and doors began to open for him. The illusion of ambitious appointments had settled upon his life and the quest for answers which had begun to open up his mind, was cast aside.

Pride had begun to work effectively enough, and though a more discerning mind might see beyond the distractions, Uriel could not. He'd been given a glimpse of something magnificent but closed the door before he could peel back the first few layers of its meaning. And so, darkness had won. For now.

8

The Diamond in a Bed of Roses

Darkness was the unconquered king in the sanctuary. It was an invisible darkness and because it was impossible to see, the hosts didn't even realize it was there. Just as the equal sharing of day and night gave the sanctuary its balance, the invisible darkness had to share its kingdom with the invisible light – but not by choice. By nature, darkness was all consuming. Its very nature was to seep into the smallest cracks and pour itself wherever it could. If a host allowed it, darkness would consume and ultimately destroy him. But darkness could not consume the spirit, because it was made of light. So if a host chose to be consumed by darkness, the only escape for a spirit was through the death of the host. And under the great weight of darkness, many hosts contemplated the idea of death as an escape.

Ai knew it would be difficult for spirits in LIFE because they had to endure a constant battle and they would have to continually resist darkness through the entire journey. The pearls in the hand of darkness would ultimately mold each spirit into a shape, like a cup or vessel that could contain the most beautiful light imaginable. And this was the purpose. Ai never created anything without the possibility of expansion, and LIFE offered an abundance of fertile ground for growth. Darkness was like the earth itself, into which seeds of light were injected. The dark earth would force them to erupt and break through, and expand into a potential far beyond their original shape and size, and even exceed far beyond their original beauty. It would force everything to change. Such was the nature of the darkest earth – that it could spawn miraculous growth!

The hosts valued their stories, and Ai designed everything in LIFE to contain a story to reflect the truth of creation. And just as the sun and moon shared their time equally in the sanctuary, so the invisible all consuming darkness had to accept the reality of the invisible, timeless light.

In his mind Uriel possessed great knowledge about many things. But he had always lived through his mind and what he learned from the five sensations. He was able to understand that. Aquilo lived by his spirit which Uriel was afraid to do. He didn't know it was fear, but it certainly was the cause for his hesitation to move forward on this new unfamiliar path. Fear was what caused him to resist that which was foreign, because fear of the unknown was the root cause of strife in the sanctuary.

Fear was behind the hesitation that everyone felt in LIFE about moving toward the light. It wasn't that they didn't want to go in that direction, but more because they were creatures of habit and darkness was familiar. They had become comfortable, as much as one could, living in darkness. Although they entertained the idea of escape, most didn't do more than talk about it now and then.

Uriel needed to learn to allow himself to be led by his spirit more as well as his mind, just like the days and nights each took their turn ruling the sky. His mind was formed in darkness but his spirit was made from light. Balance could only come to Uriel's life when he learned to achieve a balance within himself. Until now, Uriel's mind had directed him and the danger of continuing on that path was that the darkness within could gain more control. Darkness always resisted change and it pressed Uriel to be doubtful and suspicious of any form of light.

Naturally all imperative battles in LIFE were fought in the mind: between all consuming darkness, and all consuming light. Although the hosts didn't consciously think about it, they were drawn to that recurring struggle in all the stories that filled their cultures and entertained them.

Over a year had passed since Uriel returned home from his excursion to the north. The vision of the ice crystals still appeared whenever he first closed his eyes but, as time passed, darkness lured his attention away to other images and the deep impression of the north began to fade. And he began to feel that he should subdue his curiosity for fear of what pursuing the light might cost him. The pursuit of light was actually the path to freedom and fulfillment and darkness knew well the importance of blinding him from that fact. It also knew the gains to be had by creeping ever so slowly to avoid detection entirely. For no one would reject an undetected enemy. And so the host could be consumed by degrees, over a long period of time, and never even know.

One day, on his way home, Uriel stopped off at a convenience store to pick up a few things. He parked on the side of the street and went inside. A few moments later he came out, walked around to the front door of his car clicking his remote to unlock it. Suddenly he had a pressing thought in his mind urging him to go back into the store for something. Without another thought he walked back around his car and just as he reached out to grab the door at the front of the store he stopped, asking himself,

"What am I doing? I don't need anything else." So he turned around. But at that very instant he turned to see a heavy cement truck, completely out of control as it swerved back and forth and smashed into his car, completely crushing the driver's side. Uriel froze. The loud crashing sound of the truck hitting his car so quickly struck fear into his heart. He felt faint. After a few minutes, when other people came running out to see what happened, Uriel walked slowly around to the front of his car. The truck had swerved out again and was stopped a few hundred feet down the street. No other cars parked along that street had been hit – just his. As he looked at the driver's side his heart was pounding. He could see himself in the driver's seat, which was completely smashed in, almost over to the passenger's side. That would have been him, dead for sure. People were fussing about, shocked and amazed at the damage. Uriel sank back. He felt dizzy and had to lean against the wall of the building. His thoughts were racing and his mind began to swim in a sea of questions.

The rest of the afternoon was a blur. He went through the accident report with the police but found it difficult to focus on their questions. That night Uriel's thoughts kept bringing him back to one single question: "What just happened?" Clearly something had saved his life that day, and although he wasn't sure how, he knew it had something to do with what Aquilo tried to show him.

When Uriel closed his eyes that night, all he saw over and over was the truck smashing into his car. Every time he saw the image and heard the crunching sound of metal, he winced. After several sleepless hours, he got up and started to search frantically through his drawers. Finally in the bottom drawer he found the pouch. He unwrapped the crystal and focused on it, thinking that maybe if he concentrated hard enough he would be able to decipher its message. Still nothing. He'd looked at it so many times before with no idea what he was looking for. And still it offered no clues.

Finally Uriel fell asleep with the crystal still in his hand. And this time the visions in his head were once again about the magnificent ice cave. His heart rate slowed and he drifted into a deep relaxed sleep. His dreams were in vivid color that night. He was with Aquilo at the ice crystal cave again, only this time the prisms of colour from the ice ranged in every color of the rainbow. Glowing hues danced on the walls of the cave and on their faces. Then Uriel looked at the waterfall and suddenly he and Aquilo were standing on a hilltop, looking at a magnificent mountain, which was bare except for its white peak. Aquilo turned to him and said,

"Go to where the earth meets heaven in a bed of roses. There you will find a cold white stone set in the ring of fire. Avani is there."

Uriel woke up with the words still fresh on his mind. He jumped out of bed and went into his study. He pulled out an oversized atlas from the bookshelf and opened it on the desk. Then he turned on the lamp with its pull cord. Leafing through the pages, he came to a page showing the equator. The words "cold white stone set in the ring of fire" were running through his mind. Looking over to pull the lamp closer, he put down the crystal, which he had unwittingly held onto in his sleep. He held the lamp over the map running his finger along the equator until he stopped at a mountain range in Ecuador. As he glanced at the crystal to move it out of his way, he saw in it an outline of the same magnificent mountain that he had seen in his dream with red flecks of grain around the bottom of it! His heart pounded faster with the realization that he was onto something. Perhaps now he might finally make sense of the crystal! He picked it up and went over to his computer, intent on doing a search about the mountains of Ecuador. Pictures of the beautiful landscapes came up and then all of a sudden there it was – the same shape that was somehow etched into the center of the crystal and the one in his dream. And now it had a name – Cayambe! As he researched the mountain he discovered that Cayambe was indeed the highest and coldest point on the entire equator. It was the only place on earth where the temperature reached zero degrees Fahrenheit at zero degrees latitude. It could well be the exact place where a *cold white diamond was set in the ring of fire!* Uriel knew he had to get back to this journey. And he believed his life had been spared for that reason.

Ai, the silent observer, watched Uriel with great affection. He smiled at Uriel's excitement. He never grew tired of watching creation expand. There in the invisible darkness of the sanctuary, within Uriel, Ai could see the beauty of a flicker of light bursting even for a second. And each flicker, was hope surfacing like the first shoots from a new seed. Nothing mattered to Ai more than the growth of the spirits and their hosts. For when love witnesses the expansion of what it loves, it too expands. Indeed those moments were always exhilarating for Ai and he didn't miss any – not a single one. Darkness covered the sanctuary, but the tiny bursts of light that continually flashed in its midst, were just as beautiful to watch from a distance.

Uriel had little to guide him other than the crystal and Aquilo's words. But he was beginning to understand the value of following an unknown path that was wooing him, even though he knew his peers would think he was crazy. So he didn't speak of it and explained his reasons for the trip in much more frivolous terms. He started to make plans and decided to leave that same year in the spring. It would give him a few months to prepare. The fall semester was already almost over and it was impossible to leave now anyway.

Months passed and the winter semester crawled by. In his spare time, Uriel took up Spanish so he could get around without too much difficulty. He already knew a bit of Portuguese. He also studied the region of Ecuador and learned as much as he could about the people and their culture.

Finally spring arrived and he was ready. During his preparation for the trip, Uriel also focussed on the things Aquilo taught him. Every night when he closed his eyes, he envisioned the magnificent crystal cave and began to repeat the words Aquilo taught him. It became a routine. To his peers it might have seemed childish or superstitious to repeat such a mantra every night. But that routine strengthened his mind little by little.

In his intellectual world, the value of simple faith was overlooked. Everything was put to the test of proof. Proof consisted of irrefutable, concrete evidence. And in LIFE the five sensations were the acceptable measuring tools and anything outside that was considered unreliable and inadmissible to the mind of reason. But still, many hosts consumed by their own unanswered questions, needed to embrace faith. Indeed they were responding to a spiritual longing to return home to a place where love was sublime, and rejection and loneliness didn't exist. Uriel felt it too – the need to believe in something beyond, something that could give his life more relevance. In that need, he was simply identifying with a longing in his spirit that had always been there.

In heaven, Oron thrived in the knowledge of his own distinct and incredible significance. Just like every other spirit, he lived in love beyond measure and had complete access to the greatest powers in the universe. Repeating those words helped Uriel build a bridge between his mind and the light of his spirit. The marriage of mind and spirit was taking place and it was beginning to illuminate a path for Uriel. Focussing on the light gave him strength. The words became rooted in his mind as he repeated them, and the truth of the words was releasing his true self while freeing his mind from its limitations.

For when a host gave his spirit the freedom to lead, all the questions changed. They were no longer about what was beyond LIFE for that became crystal clear. But the questions were about living in the sanctuary – how to exist in darkness without being consumed.

Too often it was the simple faith of a child that yielded greater wisdom than a life steeped in ritual. A child believed more freely and easily, which unfortunately also made him easy prey to certain dark deceptions. But Ai treasured the young ones because they instinctively gave their spirits more freedom to shine than adults in whom darkness had already settled.

☀

It was a long flight to Ecuador, and Uriel slept most of the way. His plane arrived late. When he arrived at his hotel, which was in the south part of Quito, Uriel was so exhausted he fell on the bed and slept through till morning. He woke up earlier than usual, just before the sun poured its golden light over the city. Uriel was wide-awake, his body still adjusting to the time change. He went to his balcony to have a look at the city and there he saw in the distance, the majestic white peaks. The morning sun had already lit up the sky with a warm golden light. The scene was mesmerizing. Uriel shivered as he took in the vision and its daunting beauty. He thought of Aquilo's words, 'the cold white diamond' as he stared at the brilliant mountains. Cayambe was hidden among them.

Uriel wasted no time. He had no idea who to look for, but was able to catch an early bus to the town of Cayambe. It was about an hours drive to the sleepy town. On the bus, there were several other foreigners who seemed equally excited about going to Cayambe. Uriel wondered if they too had visited Aquilo but after overhearing their conversation, he realized their journey was of quite a different nature. They were climbers who had traveled the world to conquer its great summits. Cayambe was on their list of peaks.

As they approached the town of Cayambe, Uriel noticed row after row of flowerbeds – each full of roses! Then Aquilo's words came to mind again, 'where the earth meets heaven in a bed of roses'. He felt excited in anticipation of the adventure ahead.

Uriel found his way to the village market where locals were selling bunches of the most beautiful long-stemmed roses with unusually large blooms. He came to learn that the Ecuadorian rose was among the finest in the world, known for its large and long lasting bloom.

People had discovered that from the dust of Cayambe's volcanic fury, one could harvest some of the world's most exquisite flowers. This was another example of how something so beautiful could be harvested from an old volcano – something so dark. LIFE was abundant with energies of beauty and light produced from the fury of darkness.

Uriel spotted an older woman standing in her booth selling roses in the far corner of the market. He was drawn to her. She was native with distinct Indian features. Uriel guessed her to be in her late fifties and he could see, beyond the age, of the remnants of a once lovely young woman. As he approached, she watched him with a curious expression on her face. And without meaning to, Uriel softly asked,

"Avani?"

"And you are?" she responded, surprisingly in English.

At that moment, Uriel's spirit seemed to guide his words. He spoke without thinking, "The light is within me. It is there to guide me and show me my true self. If I so choose, my light can overcome all darkness for it truly has the power to create in me all that I can imagine.

He had repeated those words to himself so often that they flowed out of him, without thought, at that precise moment. The woman stared into his eyes for a long silent moment. He began to feel foolish for speaking at all. She turned around and called another woman over to her stall and said something to her in Spanish. Then she came out from behind the stall and walked up to him.

"You have seen Aquilo?"

"Yes."

Uriel pulled the crystal out of his pocket and showed it to her. Her eyes widened as she slowly drew it from his hand whispering,

"Cayambe!"

She turned it on its side and rubbed her thumb over the image. Her eyes welled up with tears of delight. Her LIFE journey had been filled with adventures of enlightenment that allowed her to help and teach others. She turned to Uriel and her smile sank into a more serious expression. Her present mandate became clear. She pulled his sleeve and led him through the market.

"You have begun to recognize your true self and that you must let it guide you?" She wanted to say so much more but it had only been five minutes and experience taught her the value of patience and timing. He nodded at her. Then she smiled, attempting to conceal her excitement about the adventure that would unfold from this new visitor.

"While you are here, you will rise with me every morning at dawn, and together we will greet the light. That will be a daily reminder to let your spirit guide and strengthen you. It will energize your mind and soul the way food energizes your body."

As she continued, they turned down a small street leading to a modest house, which was her home. She prepared a simple meal of bread and soup. While they sat at her little table over the meal, Uriel studied her. She spoke English remarkably well for an Ecuadorian. It was evident she had traveled outside the country. Perhaps she chose to live here because of her roots. She spoke with a lot of wisdom. Her skin was darker than the average native and her hair was black with a few gray strands around her face. After the meal, she put out a plate of shortbread cookies or 'bizcochos', famous in that region.

"I want to show you something," she continued as he gobbled up a few cookies. She got up and went to the corner of the room to pick up a small woven sack. It was empty but she put it over her shoulder. Then she motioned him to come with her.

"What's that for?" he asked as he stood up. She looked at him, somewhat surprised by his question. Then she approached him, and taking hold of his hand, she led him out the door explaining,

"If we find a treasure along the way, then how can I carry it home without a bag to put it in." She laughed. "You must always be prepared to receive a gift at any moment."

There it was – that childlike expectation of good fortune. She was intriguing. On one hand she spoke with such wisdom and on the other she had a childlike faith.

They walked for about an hour out of town into the hills. After going over a few gentle rolling hills they came to a rocky area behind which they could clearly see the great Cayambe in full view. It was a genuine sleeping volcano as were many mountains in that region. It was situated directly east of the town of Cayambe. Avani sat on one of the bigger rocks on a flat area and motioned Uriel to sit down next to her.

"In the north, you discovered the question then?" she asked him.

"Yes."

She smiled and knelt down to touch the ground. She dug her hand into the soft loose earth under the stones. It was jet black with a sandy texture. She looked over at Cayambe.

"When the earth was formed, it was given the gift of creation. Like us, the earth has been given the power to grow. When the mountain speaks, it grows. We are frightened by its rumblings and victim to its rage, but we must always respect its right to grow. And in speaking, it has given us this." She poured some of the black earth into Uriel's hands. "Earth so rich it propels every seed in its womb to expand to its greatest potential." Uriel rubbed the dark earth between his fingers and watched her eyes as she spoke. Her eyes were a rich, dark brown – like the earth of which she spoke.

"Your spirit has been cast into darkness, just like a seed into this volcanic ash. The darkness means to force you into new growth. It provides you with many catalysts, just like this soil does for a seed. If you use its thrust wisely you will excel toward your original greatness. The seed is your spirit. You must learn how to let it guide you."

"How do I actually do that?"

She studied his eyes in an attempt to measure his sincerity.

"First, you must remind yourself daily of who you are – a spirit of light. That first impression must be the most prominent one you have of yourself. Aquilo tried to show you that in the north, did he not?"

"Yes."

"And if you know the truth about yourself, I mean really know it with every fiber of your being, then that knowledge will free you from the lies and limitations darkness has sown in your mind. You must also know that your light is connected to heaven and you are never alone. Fear is a fiction created by darkness to prevent your light from having any power inside you. If you don't resist it, darkness will naturally consume you."

She stood up and began walking ahead of him and then turned around.

"You have no idea of the adventure that will unfold when you allow your spirit to guide you. The impossible becomes possible. Your mind won't believe it, but if you persist in following your spirit, then your mind also will expand."

Uriel became excited by her words. But he felt the sense that Pandora's box was opening up and there was no turning back. He knew this was a path that, once begun couldn't be ignored. It gave him a feeling of refreshment that flowed through his entire body. He felt as though he was waking up from a long sleep. And, in fact, he was.

After several hours of conversation they walked back to town. Uriel noticed Avani still carrying her empty bag. He thought it odd how she spoke with such wisdom about so many things and yet carried an empty bag in hope of finding a treasure. Did she really think a treasure would just appear in front of her? It made Uriel wonder about how true all this was, and yet, he found himself secretly hoping she would find that 'gift' as she called it. The child in him wanted to believe in the miraculous. And against the reality of LIFE as he knew it where miracles didn't really happen, he still wanted to believe. That was not an uncommon desire in the sanctuary. It seemed the younger ones had so much more faith to believe in the impossible. But hosts of every age found great entertainment in fantasy stories. As they aged, they accepted the idea that fantasy was not a part of LIFE in the real world, but it still made them feel good to entertain the stories. It was natural, for example, for many children to have a strong desire to fly. This was because in heaven, where they were from, they could fly and the feeling of it still lingered in their spirits.

The next morning Avani tapped Uriel on the cheek whispering softly,

"It's time."

It was still dark. At first Uriel didn't know why she woke him up but then he remembered what she said about getting up early to greet the sun. He got up from his little bed in the corner. His back was stiff. The mattress was thin and the frame underneath consisted of a simple piece of wood with four legs. She was busy quietly wrapping up bizcochos and fruit and put them into her bag along with a small blanket.

In moments they were walking out the door and down the road. In silence she led him to the top of a hill in direct sight of the great Cayambe. She threw out the corners of the blanket and it billowed gently over the ground. Then she sat down on her knees facing east. Uriel followed her lead and sat. She remained silent at first. Then she spoke softly.

"When you see the sun's first light, watch it expand and take in all its beauty. Your spirit will come alive and you will feel it begin to strengthen you. Just relax. Breathe in and out fully. Feel yourself expanding."

Uriel listened carefully to every word. He was so ready for this. A moment later, the sun's light flooded the sky and poured over the white peak. The mountain stood like a majestic monument with an aura of light around it. Uriel took in the incredible beauty of the magical sunrise, and felt an overwhelming sense of serenity. He realized that this same moment occurred every day without him. And he'd missed it his entire life until now. He slowed his breathing. The light intensified. In that moment, Uriel felt as if he was witnessing the dawn of creation. He felt a tremor of excitement building inside while at the same time it seemed as if a blanket of calm was lightly settling over his head and shoulders. It was the most unusual feeling Uriel had ever experienced and he could almost physically feel himself being strengthened from inside.

They stayed there for what seemed like an eternity but it wasn't long at all. After awhile, Avani took the fruit and biscuits out of her bag. Sharing food on this incredible morning seemed the most natural thing to do. Their spirits had been 'nourished' and now their physical bodies. Uriel felt the bond with Avani, not the kind that a man feels for a woman he desires, but the kind that comes from sharing a spiritual experience together with another human soul when no words are needed.

After about an hour, Avani got up to leave. She was excited and couldn't help talking incessantly about all the things she knew and wanted to teach Uriel while he listened attentively.

"Your spirit is limitless. It aches to do all the miraculous things it did in heaven – to create, to soar, and to thrive on its own energy and light. But its been restrained within you since birth and it is suppressed by your mind. And your mind has been clouded by darkness and rules over you like a relentless taskmaster – never satisfied. Now that you're learning to follow a different voice it's like learning to walk all over again. The rules are entirely different because they are not about restraint, rather release. It's like learning to navigate without driving on the road. You have to learn to read entirely different signs and markers, but once you learn, you can go anywhere without needing to follow any roads, and get to your destination much faster. There are no more restrictions to limit your thinking. There's a whole new world of experience to discover when you learn to follow the voice of your spirit instead of your mind."

Suddenly Avani stopped in her step and grabbed Uriel's hands in hers. She gave him a wide-eyed stare that reminded him of a little girl. She paused. He smiled, excited to hear what she was about to say.

"I want to show you something. Don't be afraid."

She turned him around so he was facing slightly northeast, but mostly east. She stood beside him and put her arm around his waist while still holding his left hand with her left hand. Then she started walking forward quickly with her arm pushing him from behind. As they moved faster it felt suddenly like they were being swept up by a forceful wind, much more powerful than themselves. Uriel could feel the intense pressure of a wind pushing him from behind, but it felt more like he was being swept up. He felt weightless – as light as a feather as the wind easily swept them up. The ground was moving so fast under their feet that he couldn't tell what they were flying over – land, water, grass or rock. It was incredibly surreal! Then everything became a blurr.

What seemed like just a few minutes passed, and suddenly they were standing in a clearing by a black river. Truly, they had been caught up in a whirlwind and then, without warning, ejected into total serenity. Their surroundings were entirely still but their hair and clothes were disheveled from the high speed they traveled. Uriel looked at Avani in disbelief – searching for an explanation. She just smiled and looked out over the river. In reality, they had traveled a great distance east to the Amazon River basin. They were standing at the edge of the Rio Negro, which was the upper part of the Amazon River. They could see a crooked series of connecting docks forming a walkway, which led to a hut on stilts over the river.

"That wasn't a miracle. It was you." She laughed. "Your spirit was in full control for a change."

He was speechless. There was no way in the world he could explain what just happened. No one would believe him. He hardly believed it himself.

"Your mind is telling you it's impossible, because it's beyond what your mind understands," she said as she started walking out on the dock walkway.

"But your mind lives within the senses. That's its only reality. How can it conceive of anything else – especially the potential of an infinite power living inside you?" She went out, not waiting for him to follow. Uriel watched her approach the little hut at the end of the walkway. He stumbled in clumsy pursuit, wasting no time to keep up with her.

"You're telling me that MY spirit did this?"

"Your spirit, Uriel, unlike your mind, is perfect. It can do anything. It has always been able to do anything. But you're blinded by the darkness in your mind. And your mind has dictated to you for so long, that you cling to whatever it tells you."

She walked into the hut and greeted an old man sitting inside. He wore a wide brimmed straw hat. They spoke in

Portuguese for a few minutes and then he led her outside and down a few steps to a long old boat with a small engine. Uriel followed. He was beginning to understand that he had only just scratched the surface of the idea of an incredible power living inside his very ordinary body. Was he to believe that it had been there his entire life, waiting to be discovered? How was it possible? Why had no one ever talked about this before? It sounded like the childish fantasy of a super-hero comic book – never meant to be taken literally.

All the knowledge he acquired and was so proud of seemed completely redundant now. He felt like a child learning how to decipher a new world. But at the same time he was beside himself with excitement. He could hardly contain it. He wanted shout it to the world, but who would believe him? He thought of *crazy old Aquilo,* as they called him in the north, and how people perceived him. Yet Aquilo, like Avani, understood how to let his spirit guide him and the result was so incredible. How could anyone, even for a minute, want to live any other way?

They sat in the boat looking ahead as it cut through the peaceful river. The Rio Negro was deep and dark like a black satin ribbon. It was so dark it reflected the clouds in the sky and the luscious green forest with the perfection of a mirror. The jungle was also magnified along the river's edge in its perfect reflection. As they motored along, the river wove its way back and forth through the famous Amazon jungle, and their ears were filled with sounds of some of the world's most exotic birds. The air was very still. Gliding quietly down river, Uriel noticed a large pinkish white shadow moving under the boat. He pointed to it without saying a word. Avani smiled and whispered,

"Yes, the boto." She smiled, scanning the river ahead of them to see if she could spot more. "They're pink river dolphins. They live here in the Amazon. And they're one of the world's most contented creatures."

In that part of the river, at that particular time of day, they happened to pass over an entire pod. Just then to one side of the boat one of them stuck his head up and looked around, bending his head forward at almost a ninety-degree angle. He stared at them for a moment and then let out a stuttered laugh the way dolphins do. Although he resembled a saltwater dolphin, his movements were much more pronounced by the way his head could bend so far forward in any direction.

The sights and sounds of the Amazon on the Rio Negro made it feel like the most vibrant place on the planet. They were on a small inlet off the Rio Negro but it began to open up into the main part of the river, which was enormous. The great city of Manaus, Brazil was on the opposite side of the river. It was an overcrowded inland port city of over two million.

"Where are we going?" Uriel finally asked Avani. He had no idea exactly where they were or how far they actually were from Cayambe.

"I want to show you the 'Encontro das Águas'. It's the 'Meeting of Waters'." As she spoke, the boat approached the middle of the river, which was more like a lake there. "This is where the two rivers meet – the Rio Negro, which is black and clear, and the Rio Solimóes, which is muddy brown," she explained.

As they continued downstream, Uriel noticed how the two distinct colors of water met, but they didn't merge. The light brown and black ran side by side for miles, without blending. Sometimes the colors danced and swirled around each other along the edges but they never merged. As Avani and Uriel floated over the two rivers, she spoke about the blending of mind and spirit. Uriel was beginning to see the spiritual lessons in everything in nature and how these sages seemed to literally draw their wisdom from nature in the sanctuary.

"The two rivers don't blend because they're not moving at the same speed. The Rio Negro flows at less than half the speed of the Rio Solimóes. And the black Negro is also colder. Your body carries within it your mind and your spirit. Although they both share the same host, they do not blend. Nor should they. This part of the Amazon contains two rivers within itself flowing side by side, and likewise, you contain two rivers – your mind and your spirit. If you travel far enough down river you will see that eventually the warm, faster water of the Rio Solimóes prevails. If your mind learns to yield then your spirit will guide you, and your LIFE can be adventurous and purposeful. But as the Amazon eventually finds its way to the ocean, so your spirit will ultimately find its way home."

Just after Avani finished speaking, they came to a point where the two rivers became turbulent with a flurry of fish flipping and thrashing in a frenzy at the surface. The commotion caused the edge of the two rivers to swirl around each other and bubble up. Avani continued.

"Your mind, which has guided you up to now, is not accustomed to flowing with your spirit, and like the Rio Negro it is slower and colder, but if you stay on this path, your mind will yield sooner or later. The sooner it gives way, the greater your adventure will be."

They noticed other boats giving tours at the meeting of the rivers. The phenomenon had become a popular attraction in the area. After following the seam along the edge of the two rivers for a while, Avani instructed their driver, the old man in the wide brimmed hat, to turn back.

It was ironic how Uriel once again learned so much more about himself in a strange land. But as journeys go, that was not uncommon in the sanctuary. Outward exploration in nature always led to greater inner awareness for seekers. The sanctuary was a place of continually evolving contradictions and the presence of darkness certainly intensified the journey.

Darkness was a lot like the black Rio Negro in that it tried to resist relinquishing control. It would strive to pour itself into every available place in the sanctuary particularly into the minds of its hosts. Uriel's attempt to live in the light and to be guided by the spirit would always be challenged by darkness. That struggle was unavoidable. But the objective was to learn how to live in a hostile environment and Uriel would have to persist in learning how to let his spirit lead. As he opened himself to the lessons, the light penetrated deeper into his mind, little by little, and repossessed territory from the grasp of darkness that had lived there for so long.

The trip back to Cayambe was completely different than the way they had come and to the human mind, much less miraculous. The old man, Avani's friend, brought them to another boat with a man to operate it and he gave them food for the journey back. They started up the Rio Negro. It was hot. There was no wind, not even a breeze. But the light breeze created by the moving boat brought slight relief from the intense heat. It was a damp heat so the breeze against their sweat made it feel a bit cooler. Avani was talking to the driver in Portuguese. Uriel could only understand a few words and decided to take the opportunity to relax. He moved off his seat and propped himself up against some sacs of grain and made himself comfortable enough to sleep. And he drifted off.

After a few hours, Uriel was abruptly awoken by a firm nudge. They were passing through a narrow part of the river and a huge tree was hanging over the water. As they passed under it Avani pointed up, signaling him to be quiet. Uriel looked up into the tree and didn't notice anything at first. The tree had a huge bulge on it and then he realized the bulge was an enormous snake. They passed right under it and as they did it dropped behind them into the water, just missing their boat!

"The great anaconda," she said watching it disappear into the water. "Not poisonous, but they squeeze the life out of their prey just enough to suffocate them without breaking a bone. They've been known to eat very large animals, including humans." Uriel looked around at the water to see if it was still in view. She continued, "Sluggish on land, but very quick in the water."

Uriel was now wide-awake. The Amazon jungle was as dangerous as it was beautiful. The dangers were always lurking from both man and beast. Rogue thieves roamed the Amazon. Avani began to talk about the jungle and its importance in the world.

"The entire east coast of South America is mountainous and all of its rain and snow drain into the Amazon basin which is like an enormous shallow dish sitting over the entire northern part of the continent. This jungle is the earth's great fresh fountain and there's an abundance of creatures here because of all the water in this basin. But more than the water, it has a wealth of minerals such as gold. Opportunists have come here for centuries time after time, searching for gold. You've heard of El Dorado?"

"I know the stories, but it's a myth. No one has ever found El Dorado."

"Many lives were lost because they believed it was real. They had reason to believe it was true from the stories they heard among the natives. The tales of vast quantities of gold and silver spread to explorers all over Europe dating back to the 1600's. They met Indians who possessed great amounts of gold, silver and jewels. The Indians showed them a sculpted garden filled with flowers and animals all crafted from pure gold and silver. After that incredible display, the Indians told them it was nothing compared to the riches of El Dorado. They called it a city where the streets were paved with gold. So the greedy explorers plundered their villages, and took all their gold and silver, and then tortured them to learn the whereabouts of this 'El Dorado'. But no Indian ever gave up the secret of the golden city. That was because no one could – they weren't talking about an earthly city." She looked at Uriel, searching his eyes to see if he was listening intently.

"And haven't you heard about the golden city with golden streets in other cultures of the world? Of course you have! The natives were talking about a heavenly city when they spoke of El Dorado. That's why they always gave their gold to the gods as a form of worship. And being tortured to death by the brutal invaders would only send them to 'El Dorado' more quickly."

Uriel thought about the stories he'd heard from different cultures around the world with similar themes – all directing people to the dream of greatness or riches in the next life. Avani continued,

"We are captivated by a hunger for great fortunes lost in some hidden treasure. And even those among us who have some degree of wealth are never satisfied. The hunger captivates us, and those who should have arrived never really do. The hunger is insatiable. We keep looking for finite things to fill a void that only the infinite can fill. We instinctively cling to the dream of earthly riches, when in fact it is because our spirits keep trying to get back to the light – our true home. A desire for the light is at the root of the hunger, but diluted by darkness, it gets redefined as the treasure that everyone is instinctively seeking.

We were created from light and left it behind when we entered LIFE. No amount of gold or diamonds can bring it back. And the myth of a buried treasure is a story told over and over of a prize that's always just beyond reach. It becomes an endless outward pursuit, intended to distract us – a clever ruse of darkness. Truly, the treasure is buried within us – each needing to unearth his own. Your treasure is the perfection that lies within you. Your spirit holds your pot of gold at the end of the rainbow! It IS everything you're looking for! Can you understand that?"

So far away from home, floating along the Rio Negro in another continent, Uriel found himself again on an inward journey. His ears were hearing words that fed his mind like no words ever had before. And as they did, he felt lighter as his spirit began to expand. He felt more alive and energized than ever. As Avani continued to talk about the land and its treasures, and about life, death and everything in between, Uriel found that listening to her was like hearing an orchestra playing beautiful music – both inspiring and soothing. His senses were heightened. This was due in part to his spirit swirling ever so subltly within.

His spirit knew the power of words, especially those of great value, for they struck the heart with great force. Words that were believed and repeated had a way of changing the heart and clearing the mind. Oron was hopeful at the prospect of having more freedom to expand and to guide Uriel's path. After having no room at all for so long, Oron was thrilled at the thought of being offered even a bit of it.

They traveled up-river for most of the day till early evening. The river narrowed again and soon they arrived at a fair sized old dock jutting out about twenty feet into the river. They gathered their things and stepped on the dock – it had appeared to be more secure than it actually was. On the shore there was a clearing with a small simple building to the side. Uriel noticed a dirt road in the clearing, which seemed to head into the jungle but he couldn't see an opening cut through the trees. He scanned the grounds more carefully and spotted a small airplane sitting behind the hut realizing it wasn't a road at all. It was a landing strip.

Avani told him to wait outside and went into the building. He looked back to where the boat was and noticed their boat and its driver already heading back down river. He tried to call the driver back not sure if they still needed him, but when the driver saw him waving, he laughed and waved goodbye, continuing on his way. Just as he turned around, Avani came out of the building followed by a very tall man. They walked around to the small plane and the man climbed in. Avani turned and instructed Uriel to bring the supplies that the boat driver had already unloaded on the dock before he left.

Moments later, Uriel found himself sitting in the back of the little airplane, with all its creaks and strange noises, climbing up toward the setting sun. The airplane bumped and jolted over every small draft, and Uriel grew more and more anxious. He decided it was a good idea to focus on something other than the flight so he started talking to Avani. She seemed unaffected by the questionable safety of the craft. He tried to distract himself by focusing on her. She saw Uriel's fear and stroked his hair. That simple gesture helped. It was forward, and in any other situation he would have interpreted it as attraction, but Avani was so highly esteemed in his mind now that he couldn't imagine her that way. Right now she reminded him of his mother, who had always been his tower of strength when he was scared. The memory of his childhood was comforting for the most part. His mother loved to ruffle his hair whenever he rushed in on one of his important childhood adventures. When he was hurt or troubled, she always comforted him by stroking his hair. Only the memory of her crying in the kitchen still made him feel uncomfortable. It was the first time that fear had made a deep impression on him. It had opened him up to the darkness of pain, as he watched the person he loved and needed, suffer. And although her pain was purely emotional, who could know the damage of a pain that pierces the heart? How could its intensity be measured? All he knew was that the wound was inflicted and darkness penetrated it. But any amount of suffering was enough of an enticement for darkness – intensity was a matter of time.

"You're afraid right now because you're afraid to die. The knowledge you've gained with Aquilo and myself is no match for the fear of death. That's because knowledge can never overcome fear. Fear is natural. It's part of the survival instinct that keeps us alive."

Her words were true. Ai had designed a natural code in every host, and it caused the hosts to cling to LIFE with all their energy. It was important that their desire to live remain strong enough to keep them alive – even in trouble. The experience of LIFE was an important journey for the spirits and an easy escape would yield nothing. That was why the memory of heaven was erased from their minds. It would have made the journey irrelevant. The spirits had to live in total darkness in order to expand and the truth of their reality also had to exist beyond the sensations. That was the only way for the journey to be effective. Even for those who died young, the desire to live was always strong. In every journey, the experience of darkness led to enlightenment – that was the evidence of growth. Although for some, darkness was too overwhelming, and escape became their mission.

Uriel noticed that Avani didn't experience fear. She lived in another reality.

"Then why are you not afraid?" He asked.

"It's not that I don't sense fear, but I have learned to harness it. It cannot control my mind or affect my actions. I have conditioned myself to be led by my spirit, which is not influenced by fear or darkness."

"So you're always in control of every situation?"

"Knowledge is not the same as wisdom. It can tell you about wisdom, but knowing something doesn't automatically make you a wise person. I know that letting my spirit guide me is the best way to live, but that doesn't mean I do it. Growth springs from action, not from knowledge. That's where true transformation takes place – in movement." Avani's voice was warm and she spoke softly. "It's easy to get stuck in the rote pattern of day to day living, where you become captive to darkness and all its limitations. Living that way gets to be so normal that time becomes forgettable. Everything presents a potential for conflict because darkness is tireless. But there's so much more to life than any of that. There's so much more magic than people ever realize. When we walk in our spirit, we are connecting not only to ourselves, but also to everyone's true self. And doing that, even in the simplest way, can be completely energizing. If you observe a little child who hasn't even learned to speak fully, you'll notice how excited he becomes upon seeing another child – a complete stranger. They are both animated over what is such a non-event for everyone else. Your spirit reacts the same way with other spirits. It is literally energized by each encounter even if it's for a fleeting moment. That's how it is in another dimension – in the light. And that's how it would be here if we let our spirits guide us.

Look at us. We've known each other less than two days and we're not strangers. We weren't strangers five minutes after we met – our spirits connected. They bonded immediately. And that, my friend, is how life is supposed to be. Darkness is what makes us strangers."

Avani continued to give examples of "following one's spirit" and Uriel, although tired, clung to every word. It was true. This woman who was a complete stranger to him only a few days earlier, now represented an incredibly strong bond. She had already become like a mother, a teacher, a friend, a wizard and a little girl all rolled into one middle-aged Ecuadorian sage.

Her character was as varied and clear to him as a bright rainbow over a stormy sky. Why didn't he see other people like this? And he could almost hear her voice in his head, answering that question. 'Because their true radiance is hidden under the blinding darkness.' Uriel smiled, noticing that he, himself, was beginning to think like Avani. And he liked the thought of that.

They landed on a small landing strip in the middle of the night. It was so dark, Uriel couldn't tell where they were, but followed Avani, as always, to a truck waiting at the end of the field. Uriel had no idea why the truck was even there at that hour, but he was beginning to see that things always seemed to just "happen" for Avani. Her timing was perfect. They jumped into the truck for a long drive back to Avani's house in Cayambe.

Uriel didn't realize that Avani was a highly respected "magic doctor" and many people sought her out for their troubles. She could travel quite far in the region and people just seemed to know her and offer to help her in any way. Unlike Aquilo, who was regarded as a "crazy old man", Avani's ability to 'live in her spirit' brought her great respect in that part of the world.

Uriel stayed with Avani for almost a month, rising early every morning to greet the first light under the shadow of the majestic Cayambe. It became such an energizing experience that Uriel went to bed early just so morning would come sooner. During the time spent with Avani, Uriel learned many things and began to adapt a different pace of life even in the short time he was there. He also learned about her village and met many people. The local townsfolk didn't have much but they were welcoming and content.

One day as the pair walked along the road, Avani stepped down into one of the rose beds that bordered the side of the road where they were. The fragrance of roses filled the air. Uriel noticed how beautiful and robust the roses were. Without a word, Avani took the crystal out of her pocket. She unwrapped it and held it up to the light. As they looked at it, Uriel noticed the red flecks of grain around the bottom of the cracked shape of the mountain and the crystal shimmered in the sunlight. Then he saw it without Avani having to say anything. The red flecks were roses, and he was right there standing in a bed of roses under the great Cayambe! He looked at Avani in amazement. All those months he had no idea how to read that stone and now it was crystal clear. She seemed to read his thoughts and laughed, nodding her head in agreement. They understood each other without needing to speak at all. They simply shared a moment of symmetry together much like spirits did all the time in another dimension. It was the realization that everything was connected – everything in life was woven together with perfect intent and intelligence and it was all beautifully hidden from the sensory world of the sanctuary.

As they walked back, neither felt the need to speak. They were savoring the connectedness of the moment back in the bed of roses. Awhile later, Avani spotted something shiny under a shrub on the side of the dusty road. She went to see what it was and found a pile of golden nuggets. Real gold! She looked back at Uriel, smiling, and pulled the empty bag off her shoulder. Uriel remembered thinking her childish for carrying around that empty bag. But now she was filling it up with pieces of gold that she couldn't have carried home otherwise. He started to laugh. How was it even possible that she could find a pile of gold on the side of a dirt road in such a random spot outside of town? But in fact, it wasn't as impossible as Uriel thought.

Unknown to him, there were actual huge gold deposits in parts of Ecuador and gold diggers still came there for that very reason. It wasn't uncommon for foreigners to hire locals to take them out to rivers to pan for gold nuggets and some returned with small treasures. Ecuadorians themselves were not given to 'the hunt' for great riches because that was not steeped in their culture the way it was in more 'modern' cultures. But some would hunt for a few gold nuggets when they needed food or supplies for themselves. The fact that gold was plentiful in Ecuador was not a mystery. One only had to step inside the colonial church of 'la Compañía' in Quito to see it. For a long time, it had been the most incredible church in South America because it was made with seven tons of pure Ecuadorian gold. So a pile of gold nuggets lost on the side of the road, perhaps from someone's newly found stash, was not impossible, given the nature of the region.

But to Uriel, Avani's discovery bordered on miraculous. She carried her bag around constantly, always prepared for a gift to befall her. Whether he thought it was childish or not, it seemed, in retrospect, like an act of wisdom. And yes, he realized that those with an expectation of blessing lived in a better world than those without. Her simple woven bag was a little sack of faith, and although it remained empty for most of their time together, now, in the most random way, it was filled – and with it, another lesson. Following his 'spirit' would mean he should always be prepared for a blessing. In the lesson of life, regardless of the nature of the surprise, blessings themselves, were the real nuggets of gold. But, more importantly, they had to be expected before they could be found. Uriel hadn't expected anything, nor was he prepared to find it. That would have to change.

Avani was always ready. She lived in a constant state of readiness. That was part of her way of 'living in her spirit'. So simple. So childlike. And so wonderful.

On the day Uriel was ready to leave, Avani gave him a gift. "You have brought me the Cayambe stone and in return I want to give you a garden."

So Avani gave him a rock. It looked like a very old rough rock. It was unsightly with brown spots all over its jagged crater-like surface. But she called it a garden. It certainly wasn't nearly as impressive as the crystal and for the moment Uriel felt he'd made a bad trade. But he had also come to learn with sages, things were never what they seemed and he should receive this gift with an attitude of thankfulness and expectation. And so, reluctantly, he did.

"Take this to the man on the ocean, and he will show you its garden and there you'll discover your own garden."

"Where do I find this man and how will I know him?" Uriel asked.

"You'll find Bula on the island of Yasawa." She said simply.

Uriel had a feeling this was all the information he was going to get. And he was right. That was all she said on the subject. He had no idea where the island of Yasawa was but he'd found Avani, so he knew he'd find the man on the ocean. At least this time he wouldn't have to decipher a crystal 'map', which wasn't a map at all, but really just an outline of a mountain that he had to dream about first in order to find! Uriel had no idea why things were revealed in such a mysterious way but he knew there must be a reason. And there was a reason.

Truth was like gold. It was a hidden treasure that required effort to be found. If it were too easy, there would be no value in the prize. Not only that, but the search itself was also the prize because effort and determination were the keys to transformation – for growth is the purpose of LIFE. And so, the most worthy of treasures in the sanctuary were always the hardest to find.

Uriel was effectively changing. As his faith grew on this new path, so his spirit began to expand. He knew miracles were not only possible but constant, even though, in the sight of men, they were invisible. He'd experienced the unimaginable sensation of being instantly 'transported' geographically from one place to another. That in itself was something he couldn't understand with his mind. It had happened so instantly and yet it felt natural. At the time, he didn't fully understand how amazing it was, but after arriving home and looking at a map, he couldn't believe how far he'd traveled – close to a thousand miles – in what felt like minutes. He knew there was no explanation and he could find no precedent for it anywhere. How could he even explain it? It's not like anyone would believe him. But convincing others wasn't important after all. It was far more important that the events thus far would prove something to his own mind – for that was what needed to expand.

9

The Man on the Ocean

Aside from the miracles, which were quickly becoming a part of his reality, Uriel was learning how to open himself to his spirit. He understood the first step Aquilo taught about recognizing his own light and that a hidden part of himself was what contained his true nature. Avani taught him that knowledge of truth was not enough, but he had to operate in that knowledge to bring about transformation. He was curious about what the next sage could possibly reveal and he returned home with full intentions of taking a sabbatical so he could pursue this fascinating adventure. His sabbatical was approved and he began to plan the next stage.

Not long after his return home however, he received news that his mother was very sick. She had lived in her little house on her own quite happily for many years, and he visited her as often as possible. But due to her sudden decline, he had her moved to a quaint little senior's home nearby. At first she didn't like losing her independence, but the luxury of having meals prepared and bonding with other residents became something she enjoyed. Now that her health was declining she needed more supervision. Uriel, who always felt responsible, knew he had no choice but to put off his adventure. Being bedridden was hard for her, because she had always been such an active woman. Uriel visited her every day in the afternoon and was able to take her for walks in her wheelchair. There was a beautiful park nearby and on nice days he took her out for a stroll. There were plenty of activities going on in the park and being outside in the fresh air always made her feel better.

On one of those warm summer days, they came to a park bench along the path by a shallow fountain pool. He sat down next to her on a park bench in the shade. He always brought along a bag of nuts to munch on while they watched people in the park. On this particular day, he noticed the most adorable little girl, maybe a year and a half old with a head full of light blonde curls. She looked like an angel. Her mother had just finished suiting her up for a splash in the fountain pool. She was impatient to jump in. Her eyes were wide with anticipation. It was refreshing to watch a child glean so much delight from something as simple as jumping around in water. As she ran, splashing her way in, she repeatedly looked back at her mother to see if she was witnessing the magnitude of the moment. After all, water was splashing everywhere and she was getting wet! Her mother was smiling. Of course she was watching! She loved being a mother and she knew the joy of sharing many such momentous occasions with her child and seeing her happy made it a perfect moment. Then Uriel noticed a dark skinned little girl approach the blonde angel. They were about the same size. The other little girl had her black curls tucked up in a puffy crown on the top of her head. The expression on both their faces was one of sheer fascination. The blonde one smiled in delight at the sight of this new visitor who was small like her. The other one smiled back, equally excited. They each took turns displaying their splashing patterns and copied one another's variations – laughing and splashing, never even saying a word to each other. Uriel was mesmerized. He remembered how Avani spoke about children being more in touch with their spirits when they were young. At that moment he had a glimpse of what heaven would be like – spirits passing each another, even for an instant, and both being energized by a simple, fleeting encounter. That was exactly what was happening now – an exchange of sheer delight. And laughter was the only objective – so simple. These children, who knew nothing about life, were showing Uriel something he hadn't noticed before. He recognized that the exchange between spirits was meant for joy. It was something he lost somewhere along the way in his own life. It was horrifying to think of injuring a little child, such as these, who were able to find sheer delight in the simple things. But in the sanctuary, there were those who were so poisoned by darkness that they sought to destroy whatever light they found. Darkness had no other purpose than to consume light, and what could be brighter in LIFE than pure joy?

☀

Warm afternoons in the park with his mother were a fond memory for Uriel after she died. It had only been several months from the time she first took ill. Uriel was glad he was there to share her last days with her. He was there when she took her final breath. She held his hand and squeezed it one last time as he sat by her bedside. He remembered the strange sensation he felt when she died. One minute he was with someone he loved and felt her energy, and the next she somehow disappeared inside herself and suddenly he couldn't feel her at all. He remembered the distinct feeling of holding a lifeless hand when her spirit departed. This was true, because Uriel's spirit was bound to his mother's spirit while she was alive, but as soon as her heart stopped, her spirit was free. It fled her body instantly and rushed up to the light without hesitation. The moment it left her body was distinctly felt. She was simply gone and at that moment he could no longer see her body as anything more than a reminder of the memories it held. Otherwise, their connection had evaporated with her spirit. And so, death was final in the sanctuary and no matter what the spirit had learned in LIFE, it was now free of all bondage and raced home with hardly a backward glance.

The intense sadness that Uriel felt when she died was not that she was gone, but that she had left him behind. A part of him wanted to go too. He felt lost in a world less familiar to him now. Watching death made people feel that way. And because they didn't really understand where their loved ones went, they were left feeling alienated and lost. And in fact they were. For what spirit would stay in a dark place if it had a chance to escape to the light. As long as LIFE clung to a spirit, there was no choice. But as soon as the host died, his spirit was happy to be free.

Not long after his mother's death, Uriel knew it was time to refocus. He kept the 'rock' in a glass dish on his kitchen windowsill. It was not a particularly appealing rock but it reminded him that the time he spent with Avani was real and the great adventure of self-discovery was still waiting for him.

Sanctuary dwellers were very much creatures of habit. They preferred to languish in familiarity rather than face the unknown, even if their surroundings were dull and monotonous. Darkness could lull them into a comatose state of mind, so their energy to discover new things gave way to habitual comforts. And so it was with Uriel. In spite of the incredible things he knew to be true, he fell into the pattern of comfortable familiarity and stopped moving forward.

After his first adventure with Aquilo, Uriel had done the same thing – virtually forgetting the adventure until a near death experience literally woke him up. Darkness effectively lulled him into a mental sleep. It knew how quell aspirations and snatch dreams right out of the heart. LIFE on hold was a permanent state for the most part.

Even though Uriel was already on his sabbatical after his mother's death, he hadn't made a forward move in his personal journey. Avani had already given him the information he needed. But he had fallen asleep and needed to wake up again.

One typical morning Uriel got up and went downstairs to make himself a coffee. Descending the stairs, he noticed his front door half open. Immediately he rushed into the other rooms to see if anyone was there,

"Hello? Anyone here?" There was no answer. He looked in his living room and saw an empty spot where his television had been. The stereo was also gone along with a few items from the china cabinet. How did he not hear the thieves? He couldn't believe they were in his house while he was asleep. Uriel checked the house for any more missing items before the police had a chance to arrive. He accounted for a few collectibles and some cash in a jar in the kitchen. The police took their report and informed Uriel that it was probably kids looking for valuables to sell for drug money. It was the usual scenario. And Uriel was told that the likelihood of finding them, unless caught in the act somewhere else, was remote.

After the police left, Uriel slumped down in his armchair. He still couldn't believe his house had been robbed while he was there and didn't hear a thing. He wasn't a heavy sleeper. As he sat there, he realized he hadn't even had his morning coffee yet, so he got up and went into the kitchen to make it. He leaned against the counter waiting for the coffee and looked out the kitchen window. Then he saw it! The 'rock' Avani had given him was gone! He couldn't believe it. Why would anyone take a useless ugly old rock? Suddenly Uriel felt his face get warm. He was much more upset than before. It wasn't that the rock had any tangible value, but it represented his journey and his future. And even if it did possess some mysterious power, as it might well have, now it was lost. He guessed that the kids took it as a joke and it was probably already tossed. Now he would never know the mystery of that rock. And now, he might never see the garden Avani told him about.

Uriel paced back and forth in the kitchen, forgetting again to have his morning cup of coffee. He remembered jotting down the things Avani told him on the back of his boarding pass on the plane ride home – about where to take the rock. So he raced upstairs to look for it. After an hour of searching in every drawer and on every shelf, he was out of luck. The only thing he could remember was the name 'Bula'. But no matter how he tried to search his memory, he couldn't recall the name of the island. If he could only remember that, it might be enough to find this man – perhaps even relying on his 'spirit' to help him a bit. Otherwise his journey was done. His spirit, of course, already knew the answer he was looking for, but Uriel was not listening. So Oron waited quietly.

Then it occurred to Uriel that he hadn't gotten up early to greet the light in a long time. It was something he started so faithfully after returning from Ecuador. He blamed his mother's illness for falling out of that routine. So now he decided to resume. It always made him feel so connected and peaceful.

Uriel got up the next morning, just before sunrise, and went into the room on the east side of his house where he sat on a chair facing the window. As light began to pour in, he allowed it to flow his mind. He gave thanks for his LIFE and asked for more love, which is what he learned to do at Avani's side. She would say …'if the great creator is pure love, then to ask for more love is actually asking for more of him and why would he deny us more of himself?'.

She was right. In her own words, Avani was describing the process of allowing one's personal spirit to release its light and so become energized. Some called it 'prayer'. But unlike the kind of 'prayer' that many hosts practiced, it was not about asking for things. It was about recognizing what they already had and simply acknowledging it with gratitude. And the meditation was done in the morning to energize the body and spirit for the day at hand – like daily manna. In spite of losing the rock and forgetting the name of the island, Uriel already felt better after doing the meditation. It gave him a sense of calm and that he need not worry because everything, no matter what, was exactly as it should be.

☼

In a moment long before this one, when Oron was descending into the sanctuary of LIFE, Ai had deposited a single tear into him, which transformed, as it fell, into a diamond. The tear was made from pure love and it was meant to help Oron through his journey. It meant that a seed of love was within him and within his human host. That tiny seed could give him the desire, from deep within, to do magnificent acts of kindness in LIFE. It was something Ai gave all spirits for the journey and even though many hosts didn't know of its existence within, they all possessed the capacity for incredible selfless love. Those who were led by their hearts tended to tap into it more than those led by their minds. For darkness penetrated the mind, but the heart was more difficult permeate because it contained the spirit.

All sanctuary dwellers believed that love originated and grew in the heart – the actual blood pump. Perhaps they believed this because the heart pumped life-blood into their veins and beat more rapidly when the host felt strong emotions. And without a beating heart, a host could not stay alive. But in fact, the beating heart only served to amplify the feelings that came from his true heart, and a host's true heart was embedded in the center of his mind, within his spirit. This "heart" was truly the most amazing source of his ability to love at all. For when a man saw a beautiful woman, his eyes would draw in her beauty and the vision would swirl in his mind around his spirit, sometimes going straight in. And it made his heart beat faster.

But stories of love in the sanctuary were depicted by the image of a beating heart in the rough shape of its actual appearance. And the heart, being filled with blood, was red, so red became the color of love. But the real heart was locked deep inside the mind within the spirit between the two reservoirs: the reservoir of emotions, which contained genetic, instinctive and learned responses; and the reservoir of the mind, which contained the will, thoughts, beliefs and stories. The true heart looked less like a heart and more like a diamond, just like the one Ai gave Oron before as he fell from the expanse.

In LIFE, darkness always attacked the mind first. It was a good penetration point, but in fact, its real intent was to consume the heart. Once achieved, darkness could devour a host and infect others. The diamond, although incredibly small, was enormously powerful and protected by the host's spirit, which in Uriel's case was Oron.

☀

"Yasawa!"

Out of the blue it popped into his mind as he was putting the garbage out, not thinking of anything at all. The island was Yasawa. He rushed to his computer to look it up – there it was in the center of the Pacific Ocean. It was part of a cluster of small islands at the westernmost tip of Fiji, a nation consisting of more than three hundred islands. So Uriel decided he would go to Fiji – a paradise on earth. He was thrilled! He would go to Yasawa and find Bula. His mind thought it foolish to fly half way around the world to look for a stranger on a little island, but he knew it was an appointment with destiny – one he didn't want to miss. It was a chance to practice listening to his spirit. He made up his mind and that was it. While he was making plans for the trip, it occurred to him that he had yet again wasted time putting off the journey.

"Why do I always put this aside and get so easily distracted?" he asked himself. He had no answer. There was still a hesitation in Uriel, not unlike the hesitation Oron felt about taking the journey of LIFE itself.

LIFE was limited by time. There was only so much time allotted for each journey, so it was important to use time wisely and grow as much as possible from everything. A host's capacity for growth was impressive in spite of the limiting parameters of time. But growth was always impeded by the intrusion of darkness and its schemes to keep everyone from moving forward too quickly.

☼

Silver shimmers of fish, weaving in perfect symmetry, swam through the shallow water as if they were of one mind. They darted slightly left or right on their course, but not even a millisecond was lost in their formation. Their perfect form gave the impression that every slight movement was rehearsed endlessly. How could they move with such perfection? They were so primitive yet created with a natural ability to swim in any direction as one body. No one needed to tell them they were connected. And they didn't resist it.

A warm ocean breeze swept over the waves and the sandy shore where Tahoe sat, working on his beloved old boat. It wasn't that he had to fix it as much as that he had a history with the vessel. It shared many of his personal stories and carried him safely through rough water countless times. He felt obliged to tend to its repairs, which were more frequent over time. He'd already managed to pull it up from the ocean floor when it went down in a storm. Even though the depth was minimal, Tahoe was proud to have rescued his boat. But loyalty was in Tahoe's nature – even to an old boat.

Unlike the Lapita natives of Fiji, Tahoe had light curly hair and paler skin. He grew up on the islands but went away to school and traveled extensively. His grandfather moved to Fiji from Europe to escape his arduous life in the north, hoping that the move to a paradise in the middle of the Ocean would offer a better life. And it had. The pace was slower, and life was simpler – perhaps too simple for some. In his youth, Tahoe left the islands only to find that he missed the simplicity of life there. He thought it ironic that everyone else worked so hard just to get a chance to visit paradise for a few weeks every year, meanwhile paradise was his home and he too left it, for a while. There were those who had come to his paradise to live and then left a short while later. They missed the tension from wherever they'd come. But most, who came there to live, adapted to the pace of life and preferred it.

As far back as he could remember Tahoe had always loved being around water. He learned very quickly, when he left for school, that he wouldn't be happy in life if he wasn't around water most of the time. He also knew as a young man that he possessed a keen awareness of the natural world and he knew how to feel its pulse. It was something he'd unwittingly developed from spending so much time outside in the islands.

After his education, Tahoe traveled and met people here and there who helped him to align his path. Several of the people he met were sages – and meeting them was no accident. He felt they were the only people who really understood him and were aware of the rhythms of nature to which he had always felt a strong connection. Tahoe was a deep thinker and he instinctively sensed the way everything was interwoven. The evidence of that was everywhere in nature But it was in the 'more advanced' cultures of the world the idea of complete connectedness seemed to be lost.

The natural beauty of his little paradise held many lessons for Tahoe. He learned to master his mind and let his spirit be his true compass for guidance. Living in a world of miracles was normal for Tahoe, but many of the miracles in his life went unnoticed by others and that suited him well enough – better unnoticed then put on a pedestal. That could become a huge problem. Tahoe stayed clear of the dream-weavers, preferring the safety of solitude when it came to matters of his 'spirit'. He was wary of the pride and fear that was used to control their members.

Tahoe lived with his wife, Brenna on the western shore of one of the Fijian islands. She was a native, however she had some English blood in her family background, so she was taller than average and her skin lighter than a full-blooded native.

Tahoe and Brenna operated a modest resort, specializing in all the native foods and culture. Tahoe grew up there and took over the business when his father died. He didn't involve himself too much with their guests, leaving that up to Brenna, who loved to share stories and ideas with anyone who would listen. She was one of those wonderfully warm people always endearing herself to everyone. Brenna also had a protective instinct and tended to regard everyone as her child. Sadly, in spite of her highly developed nurturing skills, she was never able to have children of her own.

In his younger days, Tahoe was completely captivated by Brenna's inner strength, realizing very quickly that he was a better man around her. Being with her also made him feel peaceful and he knew that she would bring warmth to his life. He was a wise man to know his mind so well at such a young age and choosing Brenna was one of his wisest decisions.

The guests they received were usually as much on a spiritual journey as they were on a vacation. Tahoe and Brenna believed that visitors were brought to them for specific reasons, which always became evident in the course of their stay. Many visitors enjoyed their stay so much they often booked their holidays there more than once.

Tahoe was well liked among the locals and spent time with them fishing, building and repairing huts, boats and doing whatever needed to be done. The Fijians were relatively happy in spite of the ongoing war in their government. Darkness and the hunger for power were thriving even in paradise.

Growing up by the ocean, Tahoe developed a sense of calm in his mind. Perhaps it was due to living with the constant rhythmic sound of water lapping against the land and the beauty that constantly surrounded him. He understood the delicate balance of lives weighed against each another. He had a strong sense of equilibrium and people who met Tahoe were affected by his calm temperament. Many arguments were subdued just by his presence. For others, Tahoe possessed a sense of knowing that they couldn't understand. It was actually his inner connectedness they were sensing. He was a man who knew how to listen to his spirit and therefore knew things before they happened.

One beautiful clear morning while he was untangling the knots in a net, Tahoe stopped what he was doing to feel the breeze swirl around him. He sensed something. He put down his work and went into the lobby to tell Brenna that he was going to the main land. She knew him well enough to know that look in his eyes. He had sensed something calling him and was tuned into it like a solitary listener tunes into a radio frequency that no one else can hear. Tahoe jumped into his boat and headed for Nadi, one of the larger towns on the main island of Venetu.

☀

The sun was hot. Uriel forgot how hot it could be in places like this. He walked along the tarmac, again wondering what he was doing on this beautiful island in the middle of the Pacific Ocean. He shook his head. His mind was incredulous at what he had done, yet again. Another fantasy. Another escapade. Thank

God no one knew the truth about his adventures. This highly esteemed man with such 'knowledge' was running after an answer that he could barely understand himself. But he was beginning to uncover something inside and in spite of his apparent knowledge of the world, or maybe because of it, he had to know more. He had to address the questions that plagued him. And if he was to believe that his spirit was his true self, then he needed to know how he was supposed to let it guide him.

Competition and comparison had always chased Uriel through life and he was in a race from which he felt he could not escape. Like so many, it drew him into its urgency and ignited his pride to strive to at least appear to be the strongest, the wisest, or the wealthiest. Whatever it was, he had to win, at least in his heat. He was driven, and what had begun in frustration and curiosity was spurred on by pride.

Uriel's life had become like so many others – going through the motions, without a clue what was really going on, or what this 'life' was really supposed to be. Was it about wading through the mud to reach dry pleasant spots now and then? His mind, always striving for perfection, was driving him like a cruel master. Nothing he could do would ever be enough! But a mind driven by darkness could never find rest. For darkness offered none. It sought to break a man, like a wild horse is broken into submission, giving up its own freedom to be ridden by another master for the rest of its life. And as Uriel stepped into this virtual paradise, darkness dug its heels into his mind.

Uriel pulled his suitcase off the conveyer and rolled it into the open waiting area. He had absolutely no idea where to go other than the name of the island. At the very least, he would spend a relaxing vacation in the sun for a few weeks. No harm done.

Tahoe always enjoyed traveling on the water. It was his favorite place – where he could best hear his spirit's voice. There was nothing other than the wind and water and being in that environment gave him a sense of wholeness. It was refreshing. Being on the water was like being home and he felt clarity and a sense of belonging there.

As his boat cut through the waves, Tahoe sensed the wind speaking to his spirit. It was strong and he could feel his body trembling. This always happened when there was a strong sense of purpose in what he was doing – either for a person or a situation that needed his attention. He trembled in a way that couldn't be detected outwardly. It was inside. Whenever his spirit expanded, he felt that way. It was something he didn't have to understand with his mind. It was not so much a voice, but a need calling him. He knew, beyond understanding, that he must engage in the adventure ahead and he would know, by his spirit, exactly where to go and when to speak.

And so it was. Tahoe arrived at the main dock in Nadi, guided by his spirit. Everything seemed to move in slow motion as he watched himself step out of the boat, and felt himself moving in perfect harmony with his spirit. It was completely invisible to anyone else, but Tahoe moved with a sense of purpose as though his appointment with destiny had been written in a day timer, if he'd had such a thing.

Tahoe walked along the dock to the road toward the stop where a bus had just pulled up. He waited a few minutes on the other side of the street. As the bus pulled away, there were a few people sorting themselves out. Tahoe silenced his thoughts and scanned the small group of people. Then he stopped. And there it was – his appointment with destiny in the form of a man wearing jeans and a white t-shirt. Tahoe smiled. He watched the man, who appeared flustered, picking up his bag. The man stopped to scan his surroundings, but didn't notice Tahoe watching him.

Tahoe stood motionlessly. He was good at waiting. If it could be said that one had a gift of waiting, Tahoe had it. He was never led by anxiety. He never rushed anywhere and yet he seemed to always be ahead of everyone else. Tahoe had mastered the art of abiding. That talent saved him from many troubles. It was something most people weren't very good at doing. Tahoe knew the secret of letting things come to him when they were ready. It wasn't that he was waiting for things to happen to him, but he had learned to move forward, at an almost perfect pace, allowing things to flow into his path at the right moment. One of the benefits enjoyed by following his spirit was that incredible sense of connectedness – like the dance of a school of fish or the beautiful music of a well-rehearsed orchestra. And in that dance, he was never lonely even when he was alone, which was often.

Tahoe was similar to Aesop's turtle in the race with the hare. He understood the value of perfect timing and he needed only to be concerned with the rhythm of his own step and no one else's. That understanding gave him the ability to outlast everyone. Others were always running in every direction, only to arrive at another dead end and become weary from a plethora of poor choices. Tahoe knew that to rush ahead when fear, anger or any dark emotion was guiding him was, in reality, going backwards and would produce not only wasted time, but more pain and suffering. He understood the rhythm of natural timing, which was key to making right choices. Just as a baby is first conceived then born only after a time of growth has passed, likewise, new seeds of understanding needed to develop fully before they could be harvested. Those who tried to run prematurely inevitably failed. Time had a blunt way of teaching all life forms that it must be respected. But time was a parameter in LIFE that didn't exist in heaven. And because those who lived in the sanctuary were completely subject to the confines of time, they didn't even consider that they could master it. But their spirits, although inhibited in many ways, had a complete disregard for the restrictions of time. And those who were led by their spirits, such as Tahoe and Avani, paid no attention to time and its regulatory role in LIFE. And remarkably, their appointments with destiny were never missed.

Uriel grabbed his backpack, which was suitable for his adventures, and started walking toward a small building near the dock. He was walking in the exact opposite direction from where Tahoe was standing. Suddenly two little boys came running around the corner, laughing and chasing each other and they ran right into Uriel. He caught the one little boy to keep him from falling when the second barreled into them. The boys laughed and in seconds continued on with their chase. Uriel watched them run behind him and as they ran past Tahoe, Uriel saw him. Uriel was immediately relieved at the sight of the fair-haired local in Fiji, thinking he might be a seasoned tourist who could help him. Without his 'rock' from Avani, Uriel felt at a disadvantage. He hoped it wouldn't prevent him from finding the man on the ocean.

Uriel approached Tahoe, greeting him with a smile.

"Uh...hello. I'm wondering if you could help me."

"That's why I'm here." replied Tahoe with clarity. Uriel took it as a joke implying that the foreigner enjoyed being mistaken for a local. He laughed and looked toward the marina and back at Tahoe.

"I need to get to the island of Yasawa. Do you know which boat goes there?"

"My boat will take you there."

"Great! How much?"

"Well, I live there, and I am on my way back. I just have to get a few things if you want to wait here. Give me fifteen minutes." Tahoe walked away, but turned back as he was leaving, "I'm Tahoe. Welcome to Fiji!" Uriel didn't have a chance to introduce himself, before the stranger went down a little side street to the shops. Uriel relaxed a bit more. Assessing the situation, his trip thus far wasn't going too badly. He sat on a bench by the dock and watched people. There were other tourists here and there but Uriel was surprised to see how few had come to visit such a beautiful place. He was right. The number of tourists was lower than usual due to political unrest in Fiji, but it was also because there were so many islands to stay on that tourists were spread out.

The sun was hot, but Uriel enjoyed a welcomed breeze off the water. Fifteen minutes later his guide returned and in minutes they were off in his little boat. Uriel sat quietly at the bow, saying nothing at first.

"Where are you staying on the Yasawas?" Tahoe asked.

"At a place on Waya – The Waya Lailai? Actually I'm looking for someone by the name of Bula. Do you know him?" Tahoe smiled and then began to laugh.

"Bula?" Tahoe couldn't help himself. It struck him so funny he couldn't stop laughing. Uriel was partly entertained by his outburst and partly annoyed. He didn't like being the brunt of a foreign joke. It wouldn't be a good idea to be outwardly offended by this stranger's outburst. But was it really that funny? It took Tahoe a few minutes to compose himself before he could speak.

"Bula is a Fijian greeting meaning 'welcome'. It's not the name of a man. Who told you this?"

Uriel could see the humor in his mistake. But it wasn't that funny. Fijians laughed a lot and they laughed easily and as much as it might have been irritating to those more tightly wound, it was simply a way of life there. In spite of the constant political unrest in Fiji, they were generally a happy, kind-hearted people. Now that Uriel thought about it, he remembered hearing that word spoken several times since he'd arrived, but he hadn't realized it was the same as the name Avani gave him. And now that he thought about it, he wasn't sure what she said. Perhaps she meant he would be welcomed on the island of Yasawa. He was quickly beginning to feel completely foolish for even being there now. Avani told him something, which seemed so important and now it turned out to be a joke. He learned so much from her in such a short time and had grown to trust her very quickly. It was his own fault. He'd been warned his entire life not to trust strangers, but he'd allowed his eagerness to take him on this adventure, much to the amusement of these sages.

Strong desires in the hosts had a way of clouding their judgment, and their judgment grew from the wisdom they learned living in the sanctuary. But if they wanted something desperately enough they were tenacious. And they often believed in things simply because they wanted to. But their judgment was always tainted with suspicion and skepticism. Some chose to keep believing in foolish things even though they were often deceived. Others, having been disappointed a few times, became complete skeptics about anything that appeared to hold too much promise. But the truth was that every host, as a child, had a natural desire to believe in miracles and somewhere along the way they had been disappointed, as darkness ensured, and their faith in hopes and dreams became tainted with disillusionment. But the problem wasn't in having great hopes and dreams – it was in where they'd invested those hopes and dreams. They always counted on the world outside, when they really just needed to count on what they already had inside themselves. Some instinctively knew how to do this, but most did not.

Uriel was feeling disappointed and frustrated. It bothered him so much that he completely missed the beauty of paradise all around him. The clear blue sky stretched over the beautiful blue water with islands scattered everywhere. Seeing the incredible stark beauty of nature would have been enough to energize anyone. It was amazing, however, that anyone could be thrust into paradise and not be affected by its beauty. But such was the nature of LIFE. Even in paradise, they could find a reason to become vexed by their own turmoil. And such was the mindset of Uriel at that moment.

Tahoe saw Uriel's disappointment, and just shook his head. This was the very type of behavior that made him return to Fiji. People, everywhere he went, were caught up in momentary and senseless turmoil that had nothing to do with anything of value. It blinded them to the beauty they could have enjoyed and savored. And that state of unrest was fueled by a sense of want that ruled over the sanctuary – another effective tool of darkness.

"Why have you come here?" Tahoe asked him.

"I guess I really don't know."

But Tahoe knew. He was filled with words for Uriel but held back. He was a man not guided by impulse. He knew how to abide. And having that knowledge is to know that in order for words of value to have their greatest impact, they needed to be used at the right moment. And those words needed to flow together with pictures to create an unforgettable image for the listener. Tahoe was excited by Uriel's arrival even though Uriel had no idea what was in store.

Uriel's spirit had not led him astray. He was exactly in the right place and although he didn't yet realize it, he was sitting in the presence of the next sage who had already anticipated his arrival and come to meet him. This was the work of spirits connecting and igniting one another. It was an adventure of self-discovery and like it or not there was no turning back. Uriel's mind was slow to follow because it was heavy with the weight of its own interpretation of everything within the sensations. And he'd given his mind so much credit it was hard for Uriel to realize that his spirit was already so far ahead of his mind. His spirit wanted to lead him to a deeper knowledge that he'd been searching for – there he was and didn't even know it.

A whole new world of wonder was waiting for him to simply tune in to it. It was everywhere, as it always was, but all Uriel could feel was doubt and disappointment. And as was common in LIFE, he missed the beauty that day and he missed the unfolding of an exciting reality. Tahoe remained silent. Forty-five minutes later Uriel stepped off the boat and walked away from the very person he came to find – the person who could show him how to find his lost self.

So often in LIFE, that which was incredible and invisible met face to face with that which was mundane and visible – but the greater of the two passed by entirely unnoticed. So often those who walked through their journey couldn't even see the wonders that were in plain view, because they were too steeped in their own chronic state of disbelief. Yet if the invisible power of the spirit were to give up as easily as the hosts did, there would certainly be no story. And stories brought hope. Those who overcame great opposition in LIFE were said to have 'strong spirits'. And that description was exactly right. Those who allowed themselves to be led by their inner strength and embrace it, beyond all circumstances or more precisely beyond the five sensations, accomplished so much more than those who did not. And their stories were told far and wide to offer hope for other journeys.

That night, Uriel was sitting in paradise. The stars over the ocean seemed to have doubled in number from the way they looked back home. As he gazed up from his lounge chair on the patio, his mind was full of questions again. The vast universe was waiting to take him into its infinite calm. The dark sky was all around him and the sounds of the earth were like a song being hummed in the distance. Still, he heard nothing. And still, he saw nothing.

At the very same moment, Ai was watching him closely from above waiting for that flicker of light to emerge. He waited and waited. But Uriel was deaf and blind, hearing and seeing nothing. Then he spoke to Uriel,

"Wake up!"

Suddenly a brilliant shooting star shot across the sky in front of Uriel. It surprised him. It shot by and faded so fast that he felt lucky to have seen it. But then as he focused his gaze more intently on the night sky, he began to see one shooting star after another. He started to realize that the heavens were exploding with light and wonder everywhere continuously right there in front of him – completely awesome and entirely ignored. He realized that he'd allowed his circumstances to blind him. He put his faith in a silly rock and a person's name. He should have realized that the spirit needed no props. It just needed his permission to lead, and he needed to trust it. His insight was indeed right, for there were no magical icons to bring about miracles in LIFE. Not a crystal, nor a rock, nor any object in itself had the power. The power came from faith, because it was faith that gave opportunity for a person's spirit to reveal the wonder of a world beyond the five sensations – a glimpse of heaven, the birthplace of hope. And right after Ai said those two words, Uriel began to wake up. He realized his own blindness and as he contemplated the wonders of the universe around him, the blanket of doubt that had subtly fallen over his mind began to fade away. From under its shadow there emerged a fresh sense of excitement in his adventure. Uriel understood that he was in the right place at the right time, regardless of what his mind told him, and he decided then and there to once again trust his spirit and its guidance.

Hope was a powerful thing. It had a way of opening a path for the spirit to take control. And even those steeped in doubt were sometimes caught by its brilliance. For hope was exactly like a shooting star, soaring through the night sky. It burned with amazing brilliance and soared with incredible speed. It offered itself over and over to LIFE. And those who took the time to find it were the only beneficiaries of its energy.

Morning in paradise was every bit as beautiful as one could imagine. After breakfast Uriel explored the grounds of his modest accommodations. It was simpler than the kind of resort one would find in a more commercial area. But Uriel liked the simplicity and the sense of Fijian culture he felt there. He had his own little bure (cottage) and took his meals in the dining area, which was a larger bure on the south side of the complex. Uriel didn't see many other guests there. He decided to go for a walk along the beach. It was still early and he wanted to start the day feeling the fresh ocean air filling his lungs. It was a good decision and it refreshed him.

After he had walked half a mile down the beach, he saw a Fijian fisherman knee deep in the water pulling his little boat with a rope. He greeted the man and noticed his boat was piled high with something he'd apparently taken out of the ocean. Uriel approached the man asking him what was in his boat. The man didn't seem to fully understand, but smiled and shook his head emphatically saying something about "good business". It looked like a pile of brownish green rocks in all kinds of shapes and sizes. The man grabbed one and handed it to Uriel as a gift. He was happy to give it away,

"For you. Good business," he said proudly.

Uriel pretended to be pleased with the gift and thanked the man as he continued along, pulling his boat through the shallow water. Uriel looked at the rock. At that moment he remembered the rock Avani gave him. It was exactly the same except covered in bright green algae. Then he smiled. Here he was just walking along, expecting nothing, and the very same kind of rock like the one stolen was given back to him again. He had learned a lesson: nothing could be gained by all the negative feelings he had indulged in on his journey and the moment he let it all go was the moment he met with what he needed. This realization made him determined to control his feelings and allow his spirit to guide him. If he wanted to really see where this adventure would lead, he knew he must embrace it wholeheartedly, without reservation. He must not only accept what Aquilo and Avani taught him, but he would have to live it. He knew the error of thinking that he could truly live this way simply by knowing how to do it. He had to do more. He had to actively change his thinking. He had to learn to hear his inner voice and follow it. And that was what Uriel began to do. There was no sense in proving this 'faith' to be false without giving it a proper chance. So as he walked along the beach, he accepted his inner self as his true guide and he felt bound to the source of all light, calling him 'God'. And then he gave his spirit permission to guide him through that day, knowing that as he was connected through his spirit, he would open himself up to the entire universe, so it could illuminate him, even though he lived in darkness.

When he did this, it made Ai smile. He saw Uriel open his heart and allow his spirit more freedom to flow as it was meant to. Uriel was finally ready to learn more. It was time.

It was early morning and Tahoe was out fishing on the ocean. He lived near a traditional Teci village on the northernmost island of Yasawa. He liked to fish, mostly because he felt at home on the water. While he was reeling in his first catch, he felt his spirit telling him to pull up his hook and head south. Tahoe loved it when his spirit prompted him. It always meant he would embark on an adventure that always filled him with a wonderful sense of awe about life. What he was sensing in those moments, led by his spirit, was the absolute connectedness of every living thing and there was no more wonderful moment than flowing in that stream of consciousness. His spirit didn't explain anything to his mind. The task of following required trust, and trust was something that needed to be learned over time and with a lot of repetition. But the adventures Tahoe experienced every time were so amazing that they put him on a natural high for days. His sensations were elated during those times and the feeling of 'connectedness' was so intoxicating that he was drawn to it and knew never to hesitate when his spirit began to prompt him. His spirit never led him into anything meaningless for it could not. But it always had a purpose. It was made of love and always sought to expand its light in the dark sanctuary. Tahoe learned not to allow his mind to fully control him, but to give preference to his spirit whenever he was prompted. His spirit was completely opposite to his mind. On a spirit led adventure, his mind was the last to know the plan and was left putting the pieces together at the end of the adventure, in total amazement at how every single piece fit so perfectly. Following his spirit gave him, among other things, a healthy sense of humility. It taught his mind there was an infinitely more intelligent way to live that he knew nothing about nor could he control. This left him feeling humble and, at the same time, grateful to have experienced each new mind-expanding adventure.

On this particular morning, Tahoe, following his spirit's prompting, headed south. The one thing about these adventures was that his spirit never showed his mind the next step ahead of time. He had to follow its guidance, one step at a time. At any point along the adventure, if he chose to stop, there would be no more prompts. That was because his spirit needed to be granted permission to lead him, and in stopping he would virtually be denying that permission. Some of his adventures took him directly to people in life or death situations. In those situations, any hesitation on his part would have meant the difference between life and death for those he helped. Tahoe continued south, passing other islands for about forty-five minutes. He

K. A. Leeman   107

suspected this had to do with the stranger he met the day before. But he also knew enough not to presume anything.

Tahoe pulled up to the same spot where Uriel had disembarked. He spoke to one of the resort employees, who were always aware of their guests' activities especially with so few guests. Tahoe knew most of the locals on the islands. It was a small place and most of the resort operators knew each other. Tahoe and the employee talked for a while, sharing a few stories and updates of recent events.

10

Uriel's Garden

Uriel felt the sun heating up and was glad to be on his way back to the resort. Walking the last quarter of the way, he saw a man coming on the beach toward him. The man got closer and he realized it was Tahoe. This time Uriel was excited to see him. He had decided that he didn't want to miss anything he was supposed to learn and to view all encounters as part of a 'planned' design. That decision made all the difference.

Uriel greeted Tahoe with surprising enthusiasm. He was a completely different man from the one Tahoe met the day before. Uriel wanted to learn how to follow his spirit, so he welcomed every circumstance as an opportunity.

"This truly is paradise." Uriel offered. "But is it so small that I should meet you twice within twenty-four hours?"

Tahoe laughed. "Perhaps once should have been enough."

Uriel understood his meaning. He wasn't sure whether Tahoe might be the one he was looking for or if Tahoe knew of the one so he held out the rock and spoke directly.

"This was a gift from Avani."

Tahoe smiled, but not about the rock. It was because his spirit had led him so well. And although he knew his spirit was infinitely wiser than his mind, it always gave him a thrill to see a demonstration of it every time. He examined the rock in Uriel's hand.

"That's not from Avani." Uriel was dumbfounded but didn't say anything. He knew this had to be the sage because he had no idea how Tahoe knew that. No point trying to lie either.

And for some reason he felt like a schoolboy as he made a feeble attempt to defend his position.

"Well it's just like the one she gave me."

"If Avani gave you a rock like this one, it was to show you something amazing. This rock won't be so impressive. But I'll show you anyway." Tahoe smiled.

Uriel was relieved that it wasn't such a big deal after all. But he wanted to explain,

"The rock she gave me was randomly stolen by some thieves. Otherwise I would have brought it."

"How long did you have it before it was stolen?"

"About six months."

"Ah."

"What does that have to do with anything?"

"Everything." Tahoe turned and walked with Uriel back to the resort. He turned the rock over and over in his hand while he spoke.

"You hesitated. And in that, you gave darkness a chance to throw you off course. You're quick to place blame elsewhere, but the truth is, when such an adventure has been given to you, you cannot afford to waiver. A double minded man will lose everything because he does not focus on one main goal and his path will be riddled with interference and delays, until he will ultimately forgo the adventure and find himself following nothing on a journey to nowhere.

But if you choose to follow your spirit on that path and then change your mind, you will have lost your former innocence as well as the pending adventure. So really there is no wise choice once you have begun, other than to complete the course you're on. And hesitation can be very dangerous. The only time hesitation is a good thing is when it prevents you from being led by darkness. Evil does not originate from your spirit. It starts in your mind, under the influence of darkness."

Uriel was relieved. Tahoe sounded just like Avani and Aquilo. It was incredible to think they all knew each other. Uriel wondered how that had happened. Were they like the mythical Knights of the Round Table but on a global scale? He spoke his thoughts.

"So how many of you are there?"

Tahoe laughed. "More all the time."

"Why isn't there some sort of sage organization or even a publication or something? This mysterious connection between you seems a bit old world, doesn't it?"

At this, Tahoe laughed heartily. He found it incredibly funny. Uriel noticed how all the sages so far seemed to laugh easily. In spite of the incredible connection they had with the universe, they seemed to carry such a light heartedness, like that of a child, without a care in the world.

By the time he settled down from the laughter, they were already back at the resort. Tahoe invited him to go for a ride on his boat. He was going to show Uriel what was so amazing about the rock. After they set out and were on their way, Tahoe, still smiling, answered his question,

"Everyone tries to contain infinity by putting it into a box. You cannot harness infinity. And the moment you try to, it becomes finite and its magic disappears. Your spirits purpose is to guide you, and only you. My spirit cannot guide you. I can only show you how to follow your own spirit. If we tried to put parameters around the adventure of following our spirits, then that adventure would eventually become like everything else contained in the mind. And darkness would creep in. The entire point would be lost and the real adventure forgotten. That's what the dream-weavers have done. A new idea excites them and once they have embraced it, they form a system around it. Systems are controlled and they offer the potential for power, and darkness seeps into every opportunity for power. And so the new enlightened idea is already undermined before it has a chance to do anything truly miraculous."

"I'm not sure I understand."

"Let me give you an example. Let's suppose you have a choice to live in either of two countries. One country is led by a leader who controls everything you do. You don't have to think for yourself. You are told what to do and what not to do. If the leader is good, your life can be relatively good. But if the leader is evil, then your life will be miserable. Now in the second country there is no leader at all. Instead, it is a country full of sages, where everyone is guided by their own spirits. In this country, there is no need for a leader because everyone understands their 'interwoven connection' to one another and they move in unison, as do the fish of the sea or the birds of the air. There are no rules, because everyone abides by the prompting of their spirits and their spirits flow in universal wisdom. And walking in the light of that wisdom creates a response of genuine compassion and understanding, regardless of anyone's physical or regional differences. In which country would you choose to live?"

"In a perfect world, anyone would choose the second country. But that's an impossible choice. There will always be darkness in the world."

"True. But if you are led by your spirit, then darkness cannot control you."

Tahoe took pride in his boat's finely tuned motor. He cared for it well and in spite of its age he maintained it so thoroughly that it performed like a new engine. He accelerated and they went speeding over the sleepy waves. Uriel was overcome by an incredible sense of calm. It was the perfect combination of being in the right place at the right time and being in paradise. The cool, salty breeze swept over his sweaty skin.

They rounded the corner of one of the islands and approached a strand of sand about twenty feet wide separating that island from another smaller island. Rather than slowing down, Tahoe opened the engine up, turning the handle to full throttle and squeezing every bit of power out of the finely tuned machine. Uriel was a little unnerved. He grabbed the side of the boat. They raced up to the shore and as they ran out of water, they shot up into the air, over the sandbar, while Tahoe skillfully lifted the prop up, ready for impact. The engine prop spun out of the water droning with the loud whir of a spinning propeller, and in seconds they were on the other side back in the water. It was obvious Tahoe had made this run more than a few times. Some villagers on the other side cheered as the two men sped away. Tahoe laughed with excitement. It was a thrill he never grew tired of.

"Kind of a local sport around here," he said in an excited tone. "You gotta have perfect timing to get over that strand."

Uriel laughed. It was a rush, even with the hard thump of impact he hadn't anticipated. Tahoe noticed him rubbing his backside,

"I should have told you to lift up just before landing. I don't even think about it anymore. Just second nature when you do it enough times."

After a few more minutes of speeding along the coast, they came to Tahoe's modest resort. It was a Fijian style cluster of bures, much like the one where Uriel was staying. Brenna came out to meet them, and in her warm welcoming way, she embraced Uriel as she would a long lost friend. It truly was the 'bula' Avani said he would find in Fiji and he couldn't help but smile.

Brenna prepared a feast from the fish Tahoe caught and after dinner Tahoe took Uriel into the main building, which was used as a reception area for guests. The roof was thatched, like most native Fijian homes, and the décor was mostly white with natural wicker furniture. The most striking thing in the room was a large fish tank full of the most beautiful samples of Fijian marine life in every shade and hue imaginable. Uriel was drawn to the beautiful underwater landscape. Tahoe, always smiling, followed him.

"This is the garden Avani was talking about," said Tahoe from behind him.

Uriel didn't quite understand. Tahoe pointed to the many pieces of rock, like the one Uriel gave him, around the bottom of the tank. Unlike the one Uriel had, they were covered with beautiful and vibrant organisms.

"Avani gave you a 'live rock' and that rock is what brings this aquarium to life. It turns a simple tank of water into a beautiful garden. It nourishes every living thing in the tank. The live rock she gave you contained all this amazing plant life and food, which, to the naked eye, was dead. It's not dead at all, only dormant, waiting for another chance to bring life and beauty to the water. The 'live rock' you gave me was only just taken out of the ocean because it was still green, but the one Avani gave you had been sleeping for a long time.

The lesson she wanted to show you was that, like your spirit, this living garden can be dormant for a very long time. All it needs to 'wake up' is water, and one little piece of 'live rock' can sustain an area more than a hundred times its size. That is why she called it a garden – it's the ocean's garden."

Uriel examined the aquarium aquascape. It truly was every bit as captivating and wonderful as the fish it sustained. He realized he was like the rock he'd lost – sleepy and dull. And as much as he had achieved in the world he knew, his life hadn't blossomed the way the 'live rock' had. And neither had he been able to sustain life around him. He'd never even considered this new knowledge as a way to live. And while he stood there admiring the beautiful aquarium, Uriel's hopes for himself grew. He could surely do as much as a simple rock, and a lot more. He was learning, little by little, how significant it could be to allow his spirit to guide him.

✷

LIFE in the sanctuary was reduced to a race of sorts. Regardless of the focus, there was always a competition and a need to perform. And, as in any race, there could only be one winner at a time. Those who worked and lived in the realm of competition often became dissatisfied and disillusioned. They were saddled by the 'unfairness' of not being the best and if they were the best, they were beset by the fear of losing that status at any moment. Everyone was engaged in the race no matter what they thought they had achieved. But living in the spirit offered a completely different way to live – one that was never about winning at all. It was about being filled with so much life that it could nourish a person to the core and then overflow and sustain everything around it. Living in the spirit was like being a 'live rock'. It was the way LIFE should have been in the sanctuary and it was the only way through darkness. But to live that way required training and self-discipline. It involved learning to how to shun the race. And that wasn't easy to do by any means.

After spending a day together with Brenna and Tahoe, Uriel felt he should go back to his resort. He didn't want to leave, but he didn't want to over stay his welcome. They ran a small tourist business, after all. It wasn't like when he was with Avani or Aquilo, both of whom seemed to just float through life. In fact, thinking about it, he didn't really know anything about them other than they had an incredible ability to follow their spirits.

"I should be getting back now."

"Of course."

Tahoe didn't want the visit to end either. His spirit had led him to this man and he wanted to make sure he provided all that he could.

After a prolonged good-bye, Uriel hugged Brenna and walked down to the boat behind Tahoe. The ride back was quiet. It was early evening and the ocean was calm allowing

Tahoe to speed along smoothly. When they arrived Tahoe tied the boat up while Uriel thanked him for the day and stepped out. After saying good bye Tahoe smiled and asked,

"Feel like going fishing in the morning?"

"Sure."

Uriel didn't want to appear too excited, but spending time with Tahoe was the reason he came to Fiji and he would take every opportunity he could. He wanted to live more like these 'sages' and being with them was the only way to learn. His thoughts about this whole adventure reminded him of the tales he loved as a child about a 'mysterious sorcerer and his young apprentice'. He laughed at himself, remembering his childhood fantasies of how he always had to play the role of the apprentice. And now here he was engaged in a real life education to learn how to live in a way no one taught in any school. To learn the deeper secrets of life, there could be no formal education. One had to find a sage to show you the mysteries of LIFE. There was something inspiring and refreshing about learning that way. Books could give knowledge, but being an apprentice offered something more tangible. It offered reality. He could feel himself expanding spiritually when he spent time with the sages, and he felt that Tahoe, more than the others was his truly his mentor. With all its miraculous events, this adventure wasn't about 'wizardry', but more about learning the magic of life – living in an amazing realm that no one even realized was there and feeding the multitudes like the 'live rock' did. The fascinating part was knowing that the missing piece was something he already possessed. It wasn't a quest to find something out in the world but rather to unlock the treasure buried inside him. Knowing that he carried his own treasure gave Uriel a sense of peace in a way that he never felt before. Rather than being haunted by the perfection of his spirit, which always made him feel inadequate, he was learning to let go of the competition, and focus on the thought that he could learn so much more just by letting go. He was excited to spend more time with Tahoe, and for the first time in his entire life, he felt vibrant and alive. His questions had subsided and he found himself excited even to go to sleep, if that were possible, in anticipation of an unknown gift the next day would bring. Every morning could feel like Christmas morning on this journey.

Dawn and dusk on the water in paradise were identical – their difference only in the direction of light. The waves were usually calm in early morning just as they were at dusk. The sun had only just broken through over the horizon when Tahoe pushed away from shore. This was one of his favorite times of the day. The other was its exact opposite, dusk. Tahoe made a point of being on the water every day at least at one of those two times. After several minutes cutting through the water at full speed, Tahoe suddenly turned his motor off. He loved to hear the boat cut through the water in silence. He used that time to meditate by staring at the water's surface as it moved past the side of his boat. As was his habit, he would still his mind and focus on his spirit, giving it a voice simply because he stopped to listen. Over time Tahoe was better able to sense his spirit whenever he focused on the water. There was no formula for anyone else in that. His style of meditation best suited his personality. And his spirit did speak to him in his early morning glide as it did every time. It wasn't a message in words. It was through the frequency he was tuned into that was plugged into the matrix of the universe. Tahoe knew that whenever he felt it, he was living in his true self. He didn't know what was in store that day or what would happen with Uriel. He only knew that he would let his spirit show him. And that was enough. Questions and queries had no place in the flow of his spirit. Tahoe had learned long ago that questions weren't important. For even if getting answers were as simple as picking apples from a tree, they wouldn't necessarily help him navigate his way through whatever situation he found himself in. Tahoe knew that knowledge, whether it was of the future, present or past, was not enough. The adventure of living in his true self by allowing himself to be led through the most unexpected and amazing journey was what LIFE was all about. Deep satisfaction was to be found in the unraveling of LIFE, not in knowing its course. And that was true of everything. He could know all the answers, but if he did not know how to live then the answers had no value. As he allowed his true self to lead, he grew closer and more connected with all of heaven and earth. He was mining the true gold in LIFE, and all else paled in comparison.

Every time a line was dropped into the water it created a flurry of movement below the surface. Uriel didn't know if it was the due to the time of day, but he'd never seen so much activity at the end of his fishing line.

"At this rate we'll be done in fifteen minutes."

Tahoe laughed. Tahoe was always laughing. It seemed to Uriel that Tahoe was the most relaxed person on earth and he liked the effect it was having on him.

"I was never a big fisherman. Always thought it was a little boring to be honest. But here it's different. I'm not sure why."

"Perhaps it isn't the fishing that's different."

Tahoe smiled. Uriel had cleared his mind of the anxious thoughts he had upon arrival. And so he was able to experience the connectedness in that moment. Everything was simple – just the boat, the water and a friend – nothing to think about except casting out his line and reeling it in. After a moment of silence, Tahoe spoke. It was as though he could read Uriel's thoughts.

"Simplicity allows you to feel your spirit express itself, and it always makes you feel peaceful. It's the opposite of confusion, which only brings anxiety. Your spirit is simple but powerful. It has no needs and no questions. Its only objective is to move freely and expand. Whenever you surround yourself in the beauty of nature, it's easier to let your spirit expand. But a person can still be in a paradise and have his mind filled with confusion – like you were yesterday."

Tahoe paused and glanced at Uriel, who was smiling weakly. There was no hiding from these sages. They saw everything. Tahoe continued,

"When your mind is filled with worry, it cuts you off from the flow of energy going on all around you. Because everything in the universe has a rhythm, and you can't really feel it unless you're tuned in. Music is another way to release your spirit. Its melody and rhythm draw you into the flow of the universe and being in the flow will energize you. Everyone needs that."

Tahoe fell silent. He had a keen sense of timing. He knew when to speak and when to be silent. It was a skill he developed by listening to his spirit. His spirit never misled him. It was never in a rush, but it never stopped moving forward. Tahoe knew that perfect timing was not perfect because of time, but because of connectedness. And it was his true self that had chosen the pearls on his path.

Prior to the sanctuary experience, Ai had given every spirit a hand in his own destiny. Otherwise how could his experience have any true meaning? Ai knew that if each spirit participated in choosing his journey, there would be signs along the way that he knew so he could find himself again in LIFE. It was an important detail. For what life could be lived without the hope of finding one's self? The sanctuary, in all its darkness, was a place where the true self was easily lost. And every spirit had his reasons for choosing his particular pearls – they resonated within his essence. The experiences were unique to each spirit and they molded the spirit for he would experience the many shades of darkness, which were all foreign to him. Some chosen journeys were very dark, others less so. Those who chose the darkest experiences would, of course, invite the deepest holes into their spirits. So naturally they were the ones who could shine the brightest when they returned home.

Unlike in the sanctuary, there was no competition in the great expanse for spirits to be the brightest. They didn't shine to be seen. They shone to cast a greater light for others. There was no struggle to find one's lost self for nothing was lost there and every spirit was naturally brilliant without thought or intent.

Once they caught their fill of fish, Tahoe took Uriel to a spot on the shore where enormous palms hung over a white sandy beach. It looked like a perfect advertisement. The palm trunks curved so sharply they formed natural lounge chairs with palmed canopies offering just enough shade. Each man took a palm lounge chair to lie on to avoid the sun's heat and enjoy the scene of the iridescent green-blue seascape. Water in the sunlight was a reflector of infinity, and just taking in the view of it was always energizing. The two men looked toward the horizon where shades of green and blue altered at the seam between water and sky. Uriel felt inspired. He spoke to Tahoe,

"Blue is the color we use to define sadness. But when you think about it, that makes no sense at all. Right now all I can see is blue and it makes me feel so serene. Blue should represent immensity beyond comprehension. It inspires the soul. The water and the sky are both so blue and as I look out I feel like I am expanding. Looking at the blue above gives me hope, and when I look out over the water I simply feel free. The rhythm of the waves puts my mind at rest and when I smell the air filled with salt and vapor, I feel refreshed. And it's all just shades of blue. So blue, at the very least, should be the color of freedom and hope, not sadness."

Tahoe was looking out at the horizon while Uriel spoke. He allowed Uriel's words to direct his gaze, first up and then out. Then he chuckled,

"I think paradise is good for you. It makes you talk like a sage."

Uriel laughed. Then as he thought about it, he grew more serious. "Is that the point of these excursions around the world – to become a sage?"

"The point is simply to answer your question: how to be human without betraying your true self?" Uriel had never spoken about his conversation with Aquilo to anyone other than Avani. Perhaps it was the ultimate question.

It wasn't that Tahoe knew about Uriel's past or his conversations with others. But Tahoe knew how to live in a way that connected him to the entire flow of the universe that tied everything together. His spirit was bound to Uriel's just as it could be bound to anyone's. The birds of the air and the fish in the sea felt it, and even though hosts tended to move in groups as well, they usually didn't understand the dynamic of it.

The very idea of family in the sanctuary was to create a grouping so they could learn how to be connected. But the connectedness of spirits went well beyond the bonds of bloodlines. It involved everything in time and space. For although darkness ruled the sanctuary, everything created in LIFE was meant to be a dim reflection of heaven. The realities that brought wonder to LIFE in the sanctuary were echoes of heaven's realities. For every creation bore the signature of its creator even though that signature might be hidden. And as difficult as it was for hosts to put their faith in a creator, likewise, it was difficult for the creator to put his faith in the hosts. If not for the light in their spirits, it would have been impossible.

"How do I betray myself?" Uriel was stuck on that point.

"By not finding and living as your true self you betray yourself. You believe lies about yourself – lies created by darkness. And those lies sell you a false identity. Many have bought false identities and paid dearly for them." Tahoe looked at Uriel soberly.

"Imagine paying with your life for a lie?" He laughed. "It happens all the time. We follow the Pied Piper and his beautiful music and willingly dance toward our own demise."

Uriel became uncomfortable. He felt a need to find answers but he wasn't sure he liked the idea that he would have to give up who he was just to find this 'true self'. He needed clarification.

"What do you mean by 'pay with your life'?"

"I mean just that. Life is only a span of time. You can spend that time living in your false self, or you can uncover and live in your true self. But once that span of time is spent, you can't get it back. Time IS your currency. They say, 'Time is money.' And that's true but not in the way you think. Time is your currency to spend buying lies or buying truth. The insidious thing about following a lie, such as in the story of the Pied Piper, is that it will lead you to believe that it's the only way to live. The crippled boy left behind in that story feels lucky to be alive, but he is still crippled and the world in which he is left is lonely and dull. When we live in our true self, we realize that the adventure within each of us is fulfilling. It brings us happiness. There's no need to follow any outside 'pied piper', because we should each follow our own music." And almost as if Tahoe could read Uriel's thoughts he added, "And the adventure doesn't take away what you already have, it just leads you through each day in a different way. It's not about the adventure of traveling the world, like you're doing, but it's about moving forward with a sense of connectedness that energizes every day. Then everything that begins to happen to you is simply about laughter – the kind of laughter that frees you from your false self. It pushes out the darkness and allows your light to expand. Those who laugh a lot carry a lighter load. I don't mean superficial laughter. I'm talking about the laughter that comes from your spirit. That kind of laughter lights up your path wherever you go."

Tahoe's words inspired Uriel. He had so much wisdom. Tahoe was a person who lived it, and Uriel could see that living it was the only way to fully understand it.

Uriel stayed in Fiji for a lot longer than planned. After his week was over at the resort, he stayed on with Tahoe and Brenna, helping wherever he was needed. He helped Tahoe repair some roofs on the bures. One of Uriel's interests was gardening and he was amazed by the types of flowers that flourished in the south pacific climate, not at all like the seasonal variety back home. He was inspired to take it upon himself to work on the landscaping. It turned into a massive undertaking but one he thoroughly enjoyed. He thought of it as his gift to Tahoe and Brenna for welcoming him into their home. The overgrown plants and shrubs were turning into a colorful paradise under Uriel's hand and the transformation was so striking that the gardens became a curious fascination to everyone in the area. Uriel found he so enjoyed this work that he could hardly stay away from it or think of much else. He even drew up plans incorporating themes of color and variety. Working with plants and flowers inspired him and he often talked about it during evening drinks with Tahoe and Brenna on the patio. They always engaged in fascinating tales of past adventures as they sat together at the end of each day. Tahoe and Brenna enjoyed listening to Uriel talk about the gardens and how he was learning to listen to his spirit and follow its lead. It was a discipline that took time to grow just like the beautiful gardens he was creating.

"What's so amazing is that it's really just about preparing the ground and then putting each plant in the right spot. The rest is easy – just a matter of watering it every day and watching it flourish. The garden explodes with vivid colors and fragrance all by itself. Other than rooting out the weeds now and then, the entire garden expands into something much greater than what I started with. I wish life were like that!"

Almost as soon as he'd said it he realized, and Tahoe and Brenna both responded in a chorus.

"It is!" They all laughed.

Over time, Uriel began to live more and more out of his spirit. The worries and doubts faded from his mind and, like Tahoe and the other sages, he felt light-hearted and laughed more. And the more he laughed, the freer he became. Just like his flowers, he was planted in a place where he too could expand – a place where he was continually watered and exposed to light. If Tahoe and Brenna could be compared to anything, they were like a cool breeze on a hot day – easy, light and refreshing. And while Uriel was busy transforming the wild overgrown brush into beautiful gardens, he was creating a garden inside himself. The more he let his spirit lead, the more it cleared away the dark traces of a life filled with haunting questions that fed chronic doubt and fear. His spirit's light flooded every dark crevice of his mind, for his spirit was the only part of him connected to the infinite light. Uriel needed to be fully connected to his spirit in order to benefit from that light.

One afternoon, Uriel was strolling along the path, inspecting and savoring his handiwork when he stopped to look at a particularly exquisite collection of bright red flowers. Suddenly he thought of Avani. He remembered the roses of Cayambe and the parting words she had for him, "Take this to the man on the ocean, and he will show you its garden and there you'll find your own garden." And now here he was, standing in his own actual garden. It was just as she had said and more. Tahoe had shown him the aquascape that could be spawned from a rock like the one Avani had given him, but creating his own actual garden was something he hadn't considered. He knew she meant his spiritual garden, but here in paradise, one had spawned the other. Tahoe simply provided an environment for him to grow inwardly and the fruit of his growth was also evident in what his hands had created. He felt like a completely different person now, so much so that it seemed as if Avani was standing in his distant past. His heart filled with gratitude and his eyes welled up. He'd learned about his true self from Aquilo and Avani, and now with Tahoe he was learning how to live in it. But it wasn't the knowledge that changed him. The change had come with each step moving forward in what he knew to be true. The miracle of change was happening for Uriel – and it was exhilarating. Uriel's emotions of deep gratitude turned to laughter realizing how far he'd come. And the more he looked around at the paradise he'd created, the more he laughed.

Ai laughed also. Ai also knew the incredible joy of creating a garden. As he watched Uriel take part in that, he was filled with laughter, which could be felt throughout the great expanse. Light beamed into every part of creation infusing it with a brighter glow even to its outer most parts.

For in LIFE, true joy was the virtual pot of gold at the end of the rainbow and its laughter gave birth to new life – to renew and refresh a weary journey. It was a remedy for sickness and an escape from sadness all because it provided a path of light that led the way out of darkness.

Uriel understood that sustaining this new joy was something only done by allowing his spirit to lead him constantly. It was a discipline he wanted to master. Uriel had embarked on a journey from which he was determined not to wander. His former hesitation and doubt were gone and he finally understood that he could trust his spirit to guide him on an unknown path.

11

Back to the Cradle

Spirits of light had no exposure to darkness prior to their journey in the sanctuary. There, darkness was a true test of the enduring strength of heaven's light. And Uriel's new growth was ready to be tested. There were still many things he didn't understand because LIFE would never offer up all its secrets, but Uriel was tapping into a new part of himself in a way he hadn't before. And it was expanding him in every way. He felt entirely comfortable with himself and enjoyed a sense of transparency that he would have instinctively avoided before. His spirit could no longer be blinded by many of LIFE's prevalent illusions. And there was always an infinite variety of illusions to divert and distract.

One interesting characteristic of every spirit was that it was bound to truth. That might have seemed to be a wonderful thing, except when hosts were blinded by darkness, their illusions were also created in darkness. It meant they could lie to themselves and to others, but whatever wrong things they said or did were buried in their minds. And the weight of those lies covered their spirits. The only way for a spirit to free itself was for him to throw off the lies and the only way to do that was to expose them to light. And that could only happen if the host was willing to let go of them. If he was brave enough to do this, then after the initial shame of the truth exposed, he would be flooded with a sense of relief and the weight could be lifted. But if the host refused to let go of the lie, then like a seed, it would grow inside him and cause him to live in a contradiction, which would cause him to sabotage himself in some way or other. In a sense, he would destroy himself, with the help of darkness. It could be compared to a thief not caught for stealing, and although he'd gotten away with it, his mind could not separate him from his crime and eventually lead him to sabotage himself, even if it was in some other aspect of his life. Hosts who experienced this reality called it 'karma' or 'sewing and reaping'. In reality, a host's conscience was connected to his spirit. And the freedom of living with a clear conscience was another benefit to be had by following one's own spirit. For all hosts possessed a spirit of light and they could choose to follow their light or to live in the indifference of darkness. And everyone made that choice – either by pursuing truth, or being absorbed by illusions.

Ai loved the spirits dearly and it didn't matter to him whether they spent a lifetime or just a fleeting moment shining their light in the sanctuary. It was only important to shine at least once in the darkness – no matter how long or short. And no matter how dark a life was, it could always identify its own brightest moment.

One morning in paradise, Uriel woke up to a soft voice uttering his name in a whisper.

"Uriel… wake up... Uriel… it's time…"

He opened his eyes to see Tahoe sitting next to him. His face didn't light up with his usual happy glow. He was troubled. The truth was that Tahoe had grown attached to Uriel. Their time in paradise bonded them as brothers. It was time for Uriel to continue on his journey, and to do that, there was someone else to meet.

"It's time for you to go."

Uriel became immediately unsettled. These last days he felt an amazing connection to his spirit and to the entire earth. Naturally he didn't want to leave the paradise where he'd been reborn. He searched his mind for an excuse.

"But there's so much more to learn here. I'm just beginning to understand your way of living. It's too soon. I can't leave now."

"You're ready, my friend." There was no sense trying to convince Tahoe. He was not one to be led by opinions. The voice he listened to was inward and he never wavered from it. That was something he'd learned not only over time, but also over losing time in the past.

If the journey of LIFE were filled only with time spent in paradise, there would be no contrast, and contrast was what set paradise so completely apart from everything else. But true paradise in the sanctuary wasn't even a place at all. People were in turmoil everywhere and also in the most beautiful places on earth, and as Tahoe and Uriel were building a bond on that little Fijian island, the mainland was rife with turmoil as one political group struggled for power over another. It was ironic that in a paradise where the sun and sea created such breathless beauty from every perspective that it wasn't enough to keep the hosts from anger and war. The age-old struggle for power carried its poison endlessly and was rampant everywhere. And such was the pervasive hand of darkness – so extensive that it settled even in paradise.

Uriel looked at Tahoe after a thought entered his mind, which had on several occasions but seemed to evaporate as quickly as it appeared.

"How was Avani able to move at the speed of light from one distant place to another? It's humanly impossible."

Tahoe sat watching Uriel without smiling this time. It wasn't that he was serious, but contemplative. He knew Uriel wanted to live in his spirit and understanding was the door to every new truth that would be revealed.

"When you begin to live in your spirit, or your true self, there are certain changes gradually taking place. You begin to let go of tangible things. It's like a release. These tangible things can be material things you value, or they can be beliefs that limit you, or even aspirations you desire. Whatever captivates your mind will guide its direction. Living as we do, by our spirits, we have let go of the very things that our minds try to hold on to. It's not something easily done at first. It's a process. But letting go leads to a significant change. It empowers you to do things beyond your mind. Avani has followed her spirit for a very long time. And she has developed many skills along the way. Speed over the earth is just one of them. But I'm sure you were aware of others if you spent enough time with her. She never has a need for anything. Whatever she asks for simply comes to her. She never collects anything of false value, but sows all that she is given back to the earth in some way. She is perfectly tuned into the network of all life energy in the universe. Whatever is given to her is organized and then dispersed. She spends most of her time feeding hungry mouths and thirsty spirits in distant places, almost entirely unnoticed."

Uriel remembered her carrying around that empty bag. He remembered being so amazed the day she found a small pile of gold by the roadside. He also remembered how she seemed to know certain people so well, like the old man with the boat when they miraculously arrived in the Amazon. Tahoe's great admiration for Avani was evident in the way he spoke about her. Uriel's thoughts suddenly returned to the subject of leaving.

"So where am I off to now?" Uriel smiled.

"To the pit of the earth of course," Tahoe laughed. Uriel searched his eyes for the real answer. But unlike Aquilo, Tahoe didn't speak in riddles. Where could that possibly be?

"That would be hell," Uriel joked.

"What if it were?" Tahoe challenged him. "Would you still go?"

"You're serious?" Uriel's smile faded. "I don't believe in hell."

Tahoe watched Uriel become restless and uneasy. Uriel could feel that old hesitation creep back into his mind. It was the same dull fear that kept him from embarking on each consecutive stage of the adventure, but this time it came early, before he'd even had a chance to return home. Again, as if Tahoe could read his thoughts, he said,

"You won't be going home this time. You'll have to go straight from here."

"But why is it necessary to even take the journey at all?" Even as he was still speaking those words, his spirit Oron let out a sigh, which felt to Uriel like a tiny burst of light and gave him a feeling of déjà vu. It was the exact sentiment Oron had expressed not so long ago in the great expanse when he first contemplated his journey to LIFE. He'd wondered the same thing – why it was important to even make the journey at all? The answer was given to his spirit then, and he instinctively knew it in an instant. And the answer hadn't changed.

The journey would bring its own enlightenment and this next stop was already marked on his spiritual map. And instinctively he knew he'd already somehow chosen it, long before now. At that moment Uriel was experiencing a glimpse into the depth of his true self, and into the timeless secrets hidden from LIFE. Greater truth yielded greater light. That he knew. The cost weighed on his mind, but he knew it was time to stop letting hesitation to throw him off course. It would no longer guide his steps. And in that precise instant, Uriel pushed away his negative thoughts and although questions would always be in his mind now and then, he was no longer going to be ruled by them. From now on, they would be in the background, like a movie playing in the distance. He made a decision to be guided by his true self and his thoughts would have to submit. That was the choice he had made on the first morning in paradise, listening to the rough surf on that windy day. Tahoe, lost in his own thoughts, was sitting at the end of Uriel's bed. The two men sat together, each lost in their own realities. One man's mind was clearing as he swept away the debris of fear and doubt, while the other man's mind became heavier with a sense of what he knew lay ahead. Then with a serious smile, one that Uriel hadn't seen before, Tahoe made his declaration.

"I will come with you."

Uriel said nothing. Tahoe was speaking from his true self. No words could dissuade him. As much as Uriel felt apologetic for taking Tahoe away from Brenna on this journey, he was also relieved.

Tahoe made that choice because he was led to, and so he put his thoughts away and embraced the idea. It was just that simple. As wonderful as paradise was, this journey needed a contrast – as a measuring tool for growth. Tahoe knew this was the contrast so that he could return home with more than he now possessed. Whether Tahoe knew it or not, his spirit was yearning to expand through another adventure. And his spirit was his driving force.

☀

The sun poured its heat over the dry dusty road. After moving silently along the barren road leading west, then turning southward following the coastline of a huge lake, the car came up to an area of lush green vegetation, not seen since the airport. They had left the Ben Gurion airport 130 miles and several hours behind. The taxi turned into the driveway of a modest inn. The two men stepped out, grabbed their bags and went inside. Once checked in, they went straight outside to the patio for a cool drink.

"It's strange seeing you out of your element," said Uriel.

"I missed paradise from the moment we took off," Tahoe lamented.

Uriel noticed that Tahoe looked different somehow. He'd lost his relaxed glow, perhaps from the natural contentment he felt back in Fiji. Uriel was comforted to know that in spite of his inner strength, Tahoe too possessed some weakness. Knowing that brought him comfort.

They were sitting on the patio overlooking the famous Dead Sea – a historical landmark and one of curious origins. Tahoe had been here before.

"This is the lowest point on the earth. Over a thousand feet below sea level anyway." Said Tahoe.

"So this is hell?" Uriel laughed. "It's beautiful."

"Historically, this was the place of ultimate death. It's said that the skies opened up and poured down a meteor shower of burning sulfur, killing everything."

"And now?" Uriel asked.

"Now it's a place of healing. People come from all over the world with every kind of ailment and they bathe in the healing waters of this enormous dead lake. Many claim it heals them. You must try it. It's impossible to drown here. You can't sink."

Tahoe finished his drink and took out a map of the area. He pointed to a spot on the outskirts of town.

"It's around here. We can walk. It's not too far."

"What are we looking for?" Tahoe smirked for the first time since they left.

"Not what, who."

Without an explanation, he got up. Uriel followed. They walked down to the road and up an embankment. After a fifteen-minute walk, they came to a little house in the middle of a beautiful garden. Tahoe led the way through the garden around to the back of the house. Walking around, Uriel noticed a vegetable garden as well. The tomatoes were bigger than any he'd seen before. He was impressed. They were so big that at first, he didn't even realize they were tomatoes. Tahoe laughed at him.

"Yes, they're tomatoes."

Suddenly a woman's voice spoke from behind them.

"It's because we are so far from the sun down here. Our food grows that much more slowly till it ripens to perfection."

Tahoe turned around to see a young dark skinned woman obscured by a small bush next to the garden. She'd heard them clearly. It was obvious she knew Tahoe.

"Could she be another sage?" Uriel wondered. She seemed far too young to have acquired the wisdom of a sage. She was obviously younger than him, maybe in her late twenties or early thirties. While he was trying to figure out who she was, she watched him for a moment too.

"Who have you brought?"

"This is my good friend, Uriel."

"Welcome. Come inside," she announced and led them around the back into her little house.

Her house was on its own, away from the cluster of other houses in the area. As she poured them a cup of strong dark coffee, Tahoe told Uriel about Edana's background. Every once in a while she added a few words when she felt the need to clarify.

"Edana was born, in secret, to an Israeli woman. The identity of her father was kept from her and because her mother was unmarried, her situation would have brought great shame upon the family. Her father was a respected Palestinian businessman in Hebron who had fallen in love with her mother. This was unthinkable because Hebron is a place where Palestinians and Israelis have been fighting and killing each other for centuries. Although they're now segregated from each other, the city of Hebron was predominantly Palestinian. But the Jews believed it to be their region by divine right, designated historically by God himself. And the Palestinians believed it belonged to them because they had lived there for so many generations," explained Tahoe.

"My mother," Edana interrupted, "ran away from her home. And my father, her Palestinian lover, took pity on her and brought her here to this house in En Gedi. He thought her secret would be safe in this Jewish settlement. But after he brought her here, he never returned." Edana paused. There was a hole in her life where a father should have been. "I never met my father, and as a child I was told he was Jewish and was killed in a skirmish in Hebron. I believed that until the day my mother died. She couldn't die with that lie in her heart. And until that day, I'd always hated the Palestinians. They were our perpetual enemies."

She sat down at the table beside Tahoe and across from Uriel and paused for a moment.

"My mother died on my sixteenth birthday. That was the day she left me completely alone in the world. I didn't know any of my relatives. I had always taken solace in the strength of my Jewish heritage, but when she confessed to me that my real father was a Palestinian, I felt utterly lost and alone. She died in peace and left me in complete turmoil. The only thing I knew for sure was that my father was a part of me, and therefore I couldn't hate him. It was then, the lines that defined me as a Jew became blurred. Where was the difference? Why did we fight for centuries and shed so much blood? I became angry for a very long time. I had nowhere to put my deep-seated hatred for the Palestinians. But after awhile I realized my anger came from the frustration of feeling so lost. I didn't belong anywhere and I was helpless to change that. But I believe my anger was the fire that kept me alive in spite of feeling so hopeless.

It was about a year after that when I met Avani. She came to En Gedi to experience the rich minerals in the Dead Sea. Or perhaps her spirit told her to come. But the day we met, I was walking briskly, armed with my anger, ready to pounce on anyone who came too close. She stopped me and started talking. Her words were like a net and I was instantly caught. Before I could even believe it, I fell to pieces and a river of tears poured out of me right there on the side of the road. How strange it was to cry with so much passion in front of a perfect stranger! But as you know, Avani is not a stranger to anyone. Her spirit connects to yours and ...well ...she covers you like an eagle over its young."

Tahoe enjoyed listening to Edana speak, but he was too excited by this story not to interrupt.

"Avani taught Edana how to find her true self. And Edana, with her fiery spirit, learned quickly and became very strong."

Edana jumped back in taking back the lead.

"And Tahoe has brought you here to show you how to walk through the test of fire."

Uriel was fascinated. He asked her,

"What is the fire?"

Edana and Tahoe looked at each other and smiled. Then they looked back at Uriel.

"We don't know," answered Tahoe. "But for some reason, right here in this part of the world, the greatest cosmic collision occurs continuously between darkness and light. So as you allow your spirit to guide you here, the darkness will present itself to you directly and powerfully. That's when you must stay close to your spirit. Nothing else will prevail."

Edana interrupted excitedly.

"If you overcome the intense darkness here, then you can overcome it anywhere."

"But first, there are some secrets hidden in En Gedi that we want to show you," said Tahoe, taking back the lead.

"We'll start tonight," she interjected again, "At midnight. You should rest now and we'll wake you when it's time."

Tahoe smiled at Edana. He enjoyed sparring with her for the lead in telling the story to Uriel. It reminded him of impatient siblings back from an adventure, both trying desperately to reveal the juiciest nuggets of the story first to whomever would listen. Those moments of excitement were fond memories he'd had of childhood. He loved adventures, and the retelling of them was almost as exciting as the adventures had been, because it kindled his imagination and gave him a chance to relive them.

Edana enjoyed Tahoe's company. He'd always felt like a brother to her and having him around again gave her a sense of family that was missing in her young life. As Edana led Uriel to a bedroom in the corner of the house where he could spend a few hours resting, she turned and asked him,

"How is Avani?"

Uriel began to relate his experiences with Avani, and Edana listened with utmost interest.

Avani showed Edana how to connect with family, perhaps not blood-family, but one that could be infinitely more enduring. It was the family she shared eternity with – her spiritual brothers and sisters. And that family, although lost in the sanctuary, would find Edana as she learned to walk in her true self and become connected with an entire universe of siblings. Very quickly she recognized a sense of belonging that had always been there – she just needed to see it and then move toward it.

With the truth of her father's identity revealed, Edana could no longer live behind the walls she'd constructed in her mind. But in taking down those walls, she realized that she was often alone, for no one dared to even entertain the idea of brotherhood over enemy lines. In that part of the world, as in many others, the lines that divided them were as real as the darkness that consumed them.

The darkness, in its masterful ruse, used a figment of light to do its work. How clever. For the hosts were naturally drawn to light. And darkness knew that a figment of light could captivate them long enough to create an entry point. The figment of light that darkness chose was naturally the figment of heaven itself and a higher truth. That figment came to be defined as religion and so the dream-weavers emerged from among them to weave a path of division. And hosts followed, for in earnest they wanted to belong to a higher truth, and indeed they did. But darkness used the dream-weavers to lead them like a 'pied piper' and so although they believed in the light of a higher truth, they were still led by darkness.

For in all its lavish storytelling, darkness was void of one thing. The light of heaven could plainly see the most imperative element missing from every figment of higher truth in the sanctuary. And that was something as simple as love, without which every figment or religion became a heap of empty words – void of any true light. And many figments of higher truth simply withered into just that – a heap of words – leaving a tradition of patterns and rules, without substance and without power.

✺

Uriel awoke in darkness. The air was thick. Rather than feeling dry, as he should have in that environment, he felt a slimy cold chill through his entire body. He was half awake, but a scratching sound outside his door jolted his senses into high alert. He immediately went to the door and opened it. He saw nothing. Without thinking, Uriel walked outside and felt himself being led down to the shore of the salty Dead Sea. He saw something white floating a few feet out in the water and moved to the edge to get a closer look. He stepped into the water. It was cold and black. He felt a dark cold sensation move slowly up his legs. Ad he leaned closer to identify the white thing in the water. Suddenly, he realized it was a man floating upside down. It was

Tahoe! He could tell from the blond hair. But his head was immersed and he was floating motionlessly in the water. He was dead! Uriel gasped,

"Tahoe!"

Just then, a hand touched his shoulder and he opened his eyes. It was no more than a horrible dream. He was sweating in his sleep, completely caught up. It seemed so real. He looked up to see Tahoe's concerned face staring down at him,

"Hey...wake up! You okay?"

There was an almost full moon that night and Uriel could see Tahoe's pendant shimmering in the light hanging half inside his shirt. It was a carving made from an abalone shell, which bore every hue of blue and green imaginable. They were, Brenna had told him, the most prominent colors in the world – the colors of life and freedom. Brenna made it for him. She had carved a perfectly beautiful oval shape out of the shell and cut it carefully in half. Uriel reached into his shirt to touch the matching half he was wearing. She had given it to them as a symbol of their bond of brotherhood. On Tahoe's island, the two men became so close that they shared a bond very much like that of blood brothers – yet stronger. They shared a spiritual connection. Uriel felt indebted to Tahoe for mentoring him in the process of learning to follow his spirit and discover his true identity. Then the horrible dream came flooding into his thoughts and gave him a shiver.

"I had a dream," he began.

"Shhhh..." Tahoe interrupted. "Your dream is from darkness. Don't give it light. Put it out of your mind. Let's go."

In minutes they were out the door with Edana quietly leading them down to the road. They walked for about twenty minutes in the dark. Uriel had no idea where they were going. Then they came to a spot where they had to climb under ropes and down over big loose rocks. It looked like the area had been dug out extensively. They each carried a flashlight supplied by Edana. Then she motioned them.

"Wait here for a minute." She walked around to the other side of a heap of rocks and stopped. "Okay, over here." She whispered.

They walked around the rocks and came to a small clearing. Edana was shining her flashlight on the ground. Uriel could see into the light. There was a beautiful mosaic depicting peacocks eating grapes. It had something written over it that he couldn't understand. It was as if Edana could hear his thoughts when she spoke,

"The words say, 'Peace on this land'. And look at the writing below. It says that there will be a curse on anyone who causes a conflict between a man and his brother. And then below it says that no one should reveal the secret of this place to the world."

"What secret?" Uriel asked.

"The secret of a place so beautiful that the most majestic birds could wander freely eating grapes off the vine. En Gedi is the last remnant of the first garden where man and beast roamed in peace and harmony. "

"We are standing in the excavations found over thirty years ago, of a synagogue from the Byzantine period, depicting an incredible garden. And here, in this ancient work of art, is the picture of an even more distant past, far before those who created this mosaic were born."

"You're saying that this was the Garden of Eden?" Uriel asked.

"Not just this," Edana answered.

She led them back out of the pit. They walked up to the highest point. They were standing over the Dead Sea and the moonlight reflected over the water glowing with sparkles in a million flashes of light. They could see the dark outline of the Mountains of Moab across the water. It was breathtaking.

"This," she whispered, looking out over the Dead Sea. "This is the cradle of LIFE. It was once a beautiful garden in the womb of the earth – luscious and abundant. Now it's dead. No form of life can survive in its waters, and yet it continues to bring healing to the earth. In these dead waters there's healing for everyone who comes here to bathe."

Tahoe stepped forward toward the lake.

"And this is where darkness entered the sanctuary," he continued. Uriel was reminded of his dream for a moment.

"When did darkness come here?" he asked.

"It came in the form of a thought – a thought of death."

Tahoe stepped closer to Uriel.

"Darkness entered into a man when he allowed himself to think of killing his own brother – an innocent man whom he loved. Darkness divides brothers and turns them into enemies," he said.

Edana continued.

"The great creator urged him, after darkness had taken root in his mind. He said, 'Darkness crouches at your door, waiting to devour you. You must master it!'"

She turned to Uriel and searched his face.

"Those were the first words of warning given to a man directly from the creator. That should be enough to get our attention. Those words are exactly the same now. Darkness is crouching at your door with every breath you take and it is constantly waiting to creep into your mind and devour your light. You must master it!"

She stepped away from him and looked out over the beautiful moonlit waves.

"That's why you're here. That's what your journey is about – to learn how to master the darkness and follow the light that has been within you from the moment you were born. For darkness is everywhere in this world and the only way to overcome it is just as it was said to that first son, who ignored the advice and killed his own brother for no good reason. And in doing so, he started a war that has been raging ever since. He gave darkness the power to poison every weak mind. It stalks us and causes us to kill again and again. And this is where it all began. But even the Dead Sea, which kills any stray fish in seconds, continues to offer the world its power to heal. Its minerals are unique and they're sold all over the earth for their healing properties."

☀

There they stood in an oasis in the middle of the Judaen desert overlooking the Dead Sea. Uriel felt the weight of her words. He understood the war against darkness now more than ever and he was reminded again of his dream. It showed him a picture of Tahoe's death. Tahoe was his brother. He identified with Edana's story of the two brothers. He understood clearly that learning to follow his spirit wasn't just a luxury that sages enjoyed, but it was a path through darkness. It was the intended path of LIFE in the sanctuary and it was the path he was meant to discover and travel on. He also understood that death, like the Dead Sea, would bring ultimate restoration. It was a final healing place for all the misery that darkness could unleash in LIFE. But even still, before he could meet death, there was an amazing adventure to be lived, and following his spirit would uncover the greatest adventure he could possibly imagine. Following his true self would purge him of all the tentacles of darkness that had wound their way into his psyche. The path of light would set him on the course of an incredible journey and it would allow him to live in the center of his true self. What more could LIFE offer than that? And of course, laughter would become his constant companion. Tahoe taught him that.

12

Uriel's War

Ai watched Uriel and his friends standing in the cradle of the sanctuary and he was reminded once again of his own journey. He had walked upon that same ground more than once. There wasn't a trace of the abundant life that once flourished there. Darkness had long since settled into the earth's core and spread far and wide. It remained a place of constant turmoil. Uriel was becoming more intuitive as he allowed his spirit to lead. By following his spirit, he was allowing it to burn more brightly within him which, in turn, gave him more clarity and almost a more translucent glow – not a visible one, but one in the energy around him.

A translucent glow in the sanctuary was like a dim street light, illuminating the darkness with a warm shimmer. It meant that darkness wasn't able to be quite so dark wherever there was a glow. As Ai watched from another realm, his gaze moved northward up the coast of the Dead Sea. He fondly remembered many adventures along its shores. He settled his gaze for a moment on Qumran, where a nomadic Bedouin had uncovered the lost scrolls, which were filled with stories of past generations. Among them were the war scrolls. The war scrolls described, in detail, the rules of war for a generation long gone. But a truth remained hidden in the scrolls, even though they were boldly displayed for the world to see the reality of ancient battles in the sanctuary. The real battle, however, had always been about the struggle between darkness and light. And every host who would take the journey of LIFE took up arms in that battle. For just as the natives of that land fought over boundary lines and territories, so the reign of darkness, fought for domination in the territory of the human mind. And darkness was relentless. But the light would also not give up its ground – the ground rightfully given at birth in every human host. And so the natives of that land fought for centuries, simply because their stories differed without anyone stopping to consider that in the beginning they were once brothers. In stories passed on from generation to generation it was said that the first son had murdered his beloved brother for no reason. That murder started the eternal war between brothers. And after a time, they forgot why they were at war. As the battle perpetuated, the truth remained – there was still no good reason. It became reason enough to continue in the heritage of hatred that was passed down for generations.

Uriel's journey to the cradle of LIFE was to confront darkness in the birthplace of the battle between darkness and light. If he was going to take up the torch of light in all its brilliance, he had to understand the reign of darkness in the minds of men, and for that reason he was brought to the place of original death. Ironically, the first murder was not between enemies, but between brothers who lived in paradise – a garden so abundantly beautiful and grand with great waterfalls that were now only trickles in the oasis of En Gedi. It had once been a place without pain or suffering, and without fear or hatred. There was no war, no poverty and no strife. And without good reason, the first son had opened the door for darkness to enter his mind. For the mind was truly the real battleground, and that was what Uriel needed to understand. His purpose was to learn how to master darkness, just as the first son had been told to do in this very place. It was a story so old that it would have seemed more like a fairytale if Uriel hadn't been standing in this exact place.

Uriel was learning the same lesson thousands of years later. Murder was started with a dark thought and that thought was given power first in the mind, then in action. And as long as the hosts refused to follow their own light, they were helpless against the darkness in their minds.

The sanctuary of LIFE was a sacred place simply because it was chosen as the place where spirits were to take their journey. It was a place that caused spirits to expand their light and for that reason it held great value. It was the journey in darkness that would force the light to recreate itself, which was a miraculous thing. For heaven with all its perfection could not offer one thing: growth through suffering. And the only suffering that could offer real growth was to be had in the sanctuary, where darkness waged war on the light. It was indeed the perfect place.

Uriel realized that his true desire was to become a sage and he now knew it was something he had wanted for a very long time. It was that latent desire that drove him to find answers. And his desperation to find answers was what led him to discover this path. He also realized that the light he possessed belonged to everyone. Whether dormant or vibrant, it was inside every host, and it had the potential to transform his journey into an adventure of unimaginable possibilities. It couldn't be bought for it couldn't be sold. It was something that could only be sought, found, then nurtured and cultivated.

Although Uriel had no knowledge of the war scrolls of Qumran, he already knew the secret contained in its writings about the real battle between darkness and light.

Right there, hidden in a verse of the war scrolls, displayed in museums around the world, the true nature of the great battle was revealed. The words, "...and the sons of darkness shall battle against the sons of light..." were written in ink hidden in jars in a dark cave for centuries. And now these words were displayed for all to see in the light of day.

Every generation and tribe, guided by the traditions of their own stories, perceived themselves to be the sons of light. But in truth, every man who waged war against his brother was a son of darkness. And every man who sought to restore the lost bond of brotherhood was a son of light. It wasn't about tribes, stories or traditions. It was about each individual journey and whether a host would choose to be guided by darkness or light. It was about becoming a warrior of light – which was, in fact, not a warrior at all. It was about becoming a sage. Every sage knew how to follow his own light – the light he possessed since birth. And every sage understood the task of mastering darkness in his own mind in order to be a son of light. This was the adventure.

☀

The morning light in En Gedi was so bright and peaceful that it seemed to cast a glimmer of its former glory lost in another time. Uriel woke up to find Tahoe and Edana gone. At first, he wasn't concerned and enjoyed the panoramic view of the Dead Sea from a chair on the front porch. After over an hour, he began to wonder where they went and felt slighted that they would just leave without him. Then, after awhile, it occurred to him they might have left word as to their whereabouts and went inside to see if perhaps they'd left a note. Nothing. He stepped back outside the front door and then saw them walking back along the road. They were walking slowly and laughing excitedly. He had no idea where they'd been or what they were so animated about. It was at that very moment an undetected seed of jealousy entered into Uriel's mind. He knew how wonderful Brenna was and he didn't like it that Tahoe was enjoying Edana's company so much. Where did they go and what was going on, he wondered. As they approached, they noticed Uriel watching.

"Hey bro!" called Tahoe.

Uriel held his hand up in a motionless wave. They walked up the path to the house and Tahoe tossed Uriel an oversized fruit.

"Try this!" he said.

Uriel couldn't resist the only question on his mind. He had to know.

"So where did you two go so early?"

Tahoe answered, while a smiling Edana passed Uriel and went into the house. Uriel wanted Edana to stay and talk, not Tahoe.

"The market is about half a mile down the road. Edana was going and I was up, so I kept her company." Uriel didn't care what the reason was. Strangely, he became irritated by Tahoe's good humor – something he'd always appreciated before. From that moment on everything Tahoe did or said was irritating. And the more he talked, the more it bothered Uriel. The man he'd come to admire so much was now completely distasteful to him. But what Uriel didn't realize was that his mind was becoming poisoned by darkness. He'd allowed jealousy to enter his mind through his emotions and it began to unravel him like a rope straining from the weight of a heavy load. The burden of jealousy was the weight darkness used to unravel the light, and it was a weight difficult to resist. Uriel's mind filled with new questions – not the kind that had initiated this adventure, but accusing questions stirred up by pride and insecurity. What was the bond between Edana and Tahoe about? Was Tahoe betraying Brenna? Why should he bond with Edana when he had Brenna? Why did he have to take all her attention? And so, the meaningless questions took over his thoughts, and darkness crept in.

They spent the whole day exploring En Gedi, discovering waterfalls and hidden crevices that might hold secrets lost in time. As they stopped at each point, Edana described the historical events that took place there. She told stories handed down to her from her mother and all her stories were woven with bittersweet strands of joy and sadness, harmony and hostility. Although Uriel started the day feeling agitated, he became distracted for most of the day, caught up in Edana's intriguing tales of ancient times. She was enchanting.

When the sun began to sink into the western sky, Edana announced that she had to leave unexpectedly. She'd had word that a friend, now living further north, was ill and she knew she had to help. This meant, of course, that their stay with her would be cut short.

"Absolutely! Go to your friend. We'll leave in the morning. You've been so wonderful," Tahoe assured her.

Uriel stared pleadingly at Edana wanting to somehow change her mind, but said nothing. He'd grown so fond of her, but by now he couldn't even look at Tahoe. He wanted to stay but Tahoe made the decision for both of them. Uriel knew they couldn't stay and that Tahoe had done the right thing, but his agitation with Tahoe grew so quickly that he challenged Tahoe's every word, at least in his mind. And what about all lessons in wisdom he was supposed to learn here? What was the point of this journey? Was it for nothing? With each passing minute, Uriel was growing more agitated with the whole situation. What began as a spark of jealousy had grown into a raging fire of anger within him. Darkness lit the match ever so subtly and was now blowing steadily on it.

☼

Early the next morning, when they were ready to leave, Edana had also packed up her things. She'd become more beautiful in Uriel's eyes, perhaps because of the childlike way she seemed to dance around things in her haste. He saw it again this morning. She was excited because she'd prepared a little gift to present to each of them. She chose Uriel first.

"I know it's your true desire to become a sage. You will find your way only if you can learn to let your light guide you through the test of fire. You won't know when the fire will strike or where. But you must be ready. Never assume you know how to fight it. That would be foolish. Just cling to the light. For the light, and only the light, will guide you through the fire."

With that, she gave him a little gift wrapped in white tissue paper tied with a straw ribbon and accented with a small white flower. He took out the flower and pulled the ribbon. Then he unwrapped the cloth and opened it to discover another rock – a white crystallized sodium rock taken out of the Dead Sea. She searched his eyes and then spoke.

"This is a salt rock from the Dead Sea which is the earth's bed of healing. It represents the light you carry inside. Just as the Dead Sea heals all who enter its waters, so your light will heal those whom it touches. Don't let darkness consume it! For your light will guide you to your destiny." Uriel remained silent. He was honored. He understood her words clearly and they penetrated his spirit. And the darkness that had crept into his mind paused, for the moment.

Then she turned to Tahoe and presented him with a gift she picked up from the little table behind her. It was a smaller bundle, but wrapped just as Uriel's had been, except with a blue flower tucked into the ribbon.

"And this is for you," she smiled at Tahoe.

It seemed to Uriel as if her smile held more excitement for Tahoe than it had for him. And darkness edged forward.

With a silly grin on his face, Tahoe opened his gift. Uriel thought he looked stupid. His gift was a beautiful smooth blue stone, shiny and oval, about the size and color of a robin's egg. Uriel instantly felt slighted as the recipient of second place with his inferior gift. He was given a piece of salt rock while Tahoe received a semiprecious stone! How entirely unfair!

"This is your soul," she began, "You are the water that fills the dried up crevices in the earth and nourishes them with life. You are pure like the blue waters of rivers and streams. And your strength is like the waters and also solid like this stone. Follow the path of adventure that you seek and pour yourself into the dry places, where the earth is parched and thirsty. But always return home to replenish yourself. For your true home is on the ocean and it is your oasis." Tahoe laughed out loud, but as he did, tears flowed from his eyes. He knew she was right. His destiny was pouring himself into the dry places, but he also knew that his home was on the ocean with Brenna. He'd always felt torn by the choice, but now with these words, he realized he didn't have to choose at all. He now understood that both were part of his journey. While Tahoe shed tears of joy and relief, Uriel's heart burned with jealousy. He was becoming consumed without even realizing it. The hand of darkness could not be underestimated and it never grew tired in its quest to swallow up the light, especially there in the cradle of the earth. For it was in that pit of the earth that darkness had been born and so guarded its territory with tenacity!

Several hours later, Uriel and Tahoe were in a taxi heading back to the airport. Their driver was taking them northward, along the coast of the Dead Sea, following the main road, which would soon turn west toward the airport in Tel Aviv. Tahoe was quietly thinking about the things Edana said to him and reflecting on all the ways in which her words connected to different aspects of his life. Uriel was quietly seething, unable to speak because his mind was welling up with so much anger – an anger that had no good reason to exist.

Just before the road turned west, they spotted two men ahead of them at the side of the road, flagging down their car. It looked like there had been some sort of accident, because two cars were pulled to the side of the road. The driver stopped, and as he did the two men approached his door speaking rapidly to him in another language. They looked in and saw Tahoe and Uriel in the back of the car. Then, in a frenzy, they started yelling. Neither Tahoe nor Uriel had any idea what they were yelling about. Then, one of the men opened the back door and pulled Tahoe out of the car. Although Tahoe was a fairly large man, he was not violent and didn't resist. They started screaming at him. For some strange reason they hardly saw Uriel and didn't even bother with him. They pulled Tahoe down to his knees and a third man came over holding a gun, and suddenly Uriel knew this was serious. The man struck Tahoe in the face with the backside of his gun. He fell to the ground, with his face in the dirt. The taxi driver was yelling at them and they were yelling back at him and at Tahoe. They completely ignored Uriel. When Tahoe fell to the ground, he was facing Uriel who was sitting in the car, frozen in disbelief by the whole scene. While the men were yelling at Tahoe, Uriel felt like he couldn't move. He was afraid but more than that he felt a strange sense of indifference about what was happening to Tahoe. Darkness was wooing him.

At that very moment, from a place not so far away, there was another witness. Ai was watching. He stared into Uriel's eyes, searching for the diamond that had been placed there so long ago. Where had it gone? Had darkness smothered it? Watching Uriel's face, Ai shot out a burst of light – light from the great hole in his spirit that had been forged from his own journey. Then the sunlight reflected off the rearview mirror of the car and blinded Uriel for an instant. And then he heard Edana's words ringing in his mind,

"You will find your way only if you can learn to let your light guide you through the test of fire. You won't know when the fire will strike or where. But you must be ready. Never assume you know how to fight it. That would be foolish. Just cling to the light. For the light and only the light will guide you through the fire!"

This was it – the moment he wasn't prepared for! As her words filled his mind he saw the third man raise his gun towards Tahoe's head. Uriel put his hand on his chest and felt the half pendant that Brenna made for him. Tahoe wore the other half. Suddenly, Uriel knew he was being tested by the same intensity of darkness that had prevailed over the first son so long ago. It was identical. Darkness had poisoned his mind against Tahoe, his brother. And he'd aligned himself to its murderous intent – to separate the bond of brotherhood – again. Then he heard Edana's voice describing the advice given to that first son before he committed original murder: ...*darkness is crouching at your door waiting to consume you...you must master it!* Uriel knew in an instant that he too must master it. He knew that somehow in his dark thoughts against Tahoe, he'd brought this fate upon them and he had to be the one to do something.

"WAIT!" he yelled. The man with the gun looked up at Uriel in disbelief. It was as if they hadn't even noticed him before and were surprised by his interruption. Uriel knew he had to do something. As he approached the men, he asked his spirit for guidance. He was in fact asking 'God', but the spirit was his direct channel. He raised his hands and spoke,

"Don't kill him!" he said. "Take me instead. I'm the one you want!" As Uriel was speaking, he approached the men and they started yelling at him. The driver started yelling and all of them started to yell at each other. Tahoe and Uriel had no idea what anyone was saying. As Uriel got closer, Tahoe put his hand in the dirt and began to draw small circles widening into bigger circles. The second man drew his gun and pointed it at Uriel. Everyone was still yelling. Then in an instant, without warning, a gust of wind blew up from the circles Tahoe had drawn in the dirt and sand was everywhere. The three gunmen were still yelling but covered their eyes from the sudden blinding sand storm. Tahoe stood up and grabbed Uriel's arm, pulling him back to the car. By this time the gunmen were completely blinded and staggering in different directions. Somehow their driver, not far from the car, managed to find his way back and jumped in, speeding away like a bandit and still ranting in another language. Uriel looked at Tahoe's face. He felt shame for what had overcome him back there. He hid his face in his hands, shaking his head in disbelief at his own behavior.

"What have I done?" he sobbed.

"You did well, my friend," said Tahoe. "You stopped the darkness that was trying to consume you. Don't think about the ground it gained in your mind. Look at the decision you made to stop it."

"Yes, but not before you were injured," he protested. His eyes filled up with tears at the thought of the hatred that had so quickly taken over him. He didn't know where it came from and how it vanished so quickly into thin air – like a mirage. At that moment, Uriel understood how darkness could take an illusion and turn it into a real emotion – one that could commit murder. For the first time, he truly understood the real power of darkness to induce a man to create war in own his mind from nothing at all. Uriel was ashamed of himself. He was ready to watch his friend and brother, who had been so generous, be slaughtered for no reason.

"I'm so sorry. Tahoe, I'm sorry. Please forgive me. Please."

With his face still bloody from the assault, Tahoe looked at him and laughed. What a picture. All bruised and battered, and Tahoe had only laughter to offer in return.

"Though it would never have been enough for them, you offered yourself to die in my place. There is no greater love than that. And you needed to see yourself do that."

Uriel knew Tahoe had blinded the gunmen, but not before allowing himself to get beat up a little. It was important for both men to see if Uriel would be willing to risk his own life for Tahoe. And Uriel had overcome the darkness, in its greatest intensity. Tahoe smiled at him.

"You're the man I want to be!" Uriel said, with tears streaming down his face.

And there, on the northern coast of the Dead Sea, not far from the caves of Qumran, two men shared an unbroken bond of brotherhood having withstood the test of darkness.

13

Return to Paradise

Milky blue-green waves lapped rhythmically over the white sandy beach. Behind the waters moving toward the shore, dark clouds set off the ocean in a hauntingly beautiful hue of creamy aqua-green. Against the black clouds, the water was more luminescent than it was in the sunshine. Brenna was working on a special pendant for a little local boy who had helped her with jobs around the grounds. She was smiling as she pictured the boy with a surprised expression on his face as she presented it to him. Gifts were Brenna's way of showing people their uniqueness. Every carving was premeditated – cut and scraped with loving hands. There was no sign of rush in her work. She enjoyed taking the time it needed to create each gift.

She was sitting on the patio with the scene of the dramatic sky behind her, so immersed in her workmanship she didn't hear the approaching boat. Then, when it was almost at the dock, she felt Tahoe in her spirit and looked up. The first sight of her man returning from an adventure was one of her favorite moments. It was always a moment filled with excitement and she couldn't wait to hear the stories. When Tahoe saw Brenna, his heart jumped at the precise moment she jumped out of her chair. Tahoe looked at Uriel with a huge grin on his bruised face. Uriel smiled back. No words were needed. The bond had been tested and sealed. It was the penetration of darkness that taught Uriel the real meaning of their bond. And indeed, the bond of unbroken brotherhood filled him with a stronger sense of connectedness to the entire universe, even within the darkness of the sanctuary. And there, in the light of that truth, darkness was for once, absent.

Epilogue

And the question – how to be human? –
Is one that has followed each spirit
Through the journey of LIFE.
For within a host, there is a light so bright
That it confounds the mind.
And yes, that is the goal.
To seek to be ruled by light
Is to become a child of light.
For light knows no jealousy, nor hatred,
Neither loneliness nor confusion.
Neither is it ruled by darkness or fear.
But light, if given the freedom,
Leads to a path of adventure beyond imagination!

It is the ultimate path in the journey of LIFE.
But beware the darkness,
For it is tireless and sows tiny seeds of poison
Into the mind, that grow into deadly fruit.
If not cut back, a dark vine will
Creep into the heart and strangle its light.

And the master said to the boy
Who sought to be a sage:
"Darkness is crouching at your door
Waiting to devour you.
But if you follow your light
You will master it!

Notes...

The characters in this book have been given names with significant meanings to represent their identities. The four sages, encountered by Uriel, symbolize the four elements that establish the foundation of LIFE in the "sanctuary". Just as the earth exists within four elements, so the earth dwellers also possess the four elements:

Earth – flesh and bones;

Air – the breath that sustains life;

Water – that which nourishes and enriches life, and also binds it together;

Fire – the passion, whether love or hate, that drives all life. These four elements coexist with the omnipresent darkness that presides over the sanctuary.

Characters and their meanings in order of appearance:

AI *(means LOVE): This is the name given to the all powerful, all encompassing creator who is the epitome of love.*

TERRAN *(means EARTH MAN): The first eager spirit who wanted to take the journey of LIFE to gain greater light.*

ORON *(means LIGHT): This is the name given to Uriel's spirit because he is imbued with light and must fulfill his destiny – which is simply to shine in the darkness. This is a character type, representing all spirits.*

URIEL *(means LIGHT). Uriel and Oron are the same character in different forms, host and spirit, and so they share different versions of the same name. Uriel's destiny is to bring enlightenment or understanding to those in darkness. His journey reflects the journey of every human host. His character type represents the potential for everyone to learn how to shine its light and energy in the darkness. In a sense, Uriel is the reader.*

THE FOUR SAGES:

AQUILO *(means* NORTH WIND*): Aquilo represents the first of the four earth elements. He is the sage symbolizing the air or spirit. He guides Uriel into a basic understanding of his true self, which is light, but also teaches him to embrace the 'wind' or 'spirit within' in order to complete his earthly destiny.*

AVANI *(means* EARTH*): Avani represents the second of the four earth elements. She symbolizes earth. She guides Uriel through the next stage of understanding, which is how to join his spirit to the earth without being consumed by it or the darkness in it. She represents the marriage of the spirit to the earth to produce not death, but new growth – symbolized by roses. Avani demonstrates how a spirit can take on the form of earth, made from dust and live in darkness, but in that darkness, find enriching soil, filled with stimulants designed to unearth its own incredible beauty and power.*

TAHOE *(means* BIG WATER*): Tahoe represents the third of the four earth elements. He symbolizes water. Tahoe teaches the lesson of natural connectedness, illustrated by water, which nourishes and flows into every form of life. It is present in many forms, from dew and humidity to rain, rivers and oceans. Even in the host himself, the flow of water is the force connecting and sustaining his entire body. Tahoe's laughter is the fruit that comes from a soul well nourished and represented by an infinite abundance of water.*

BRENNA *(means* LITTLE DROP OF WATER*): Brenna compliments Tahoe and represents a sprinkling of water. She is the gentle prompting that a host needs to open up his true self to the refreshing and rejuvenating replenishment of water. Her role is subtle and gentle like a sprinkle of water or little drops of rain here and there.*

EDANA *(means* FIRE*): Edana represents the fourth of the four earth elements. She symbolizes fire. Edana is the only sage for whom the reader is given some history. Born a bastard child between two warring nations, she was hidden from society at an early age. Discovering that her father is the enemy, Edana is at first confused and angry in her isolation but finds Avani, who helps her uncover the* deeper understanding of her true self. Edana is the purifying fire because her path of self-discovery was induced by deep passion – hatred, in her case. She introduces the testing phase of growth. She presents a blessing and a warning before the test of fire begins. Edana's world is among the 'dead', where a tradition of war has dulled the light of its hosts. Her purpose is also to be as both the garden of En Gedi is to the desert and the Dead Sea is to the sick – an oasis of enlightenment and a place of healing for those lost in darkness. She heals and strengthens. She opens the path through the purifying and healing process. Although Edana is the youngest among the sages, she is one of the most powerful. Her deep wounds carved out a greater reservoir for her light to shine, which gives her greater power and inner strength.

www.ingramcontent.com/pod-product-compliance
Lightning Source LLC
Chambersburg PA
CBHW021233090426
42740CB00006B/510